Grateful for Everything

Steve Johnson

Grateful for Everything

Learning, Living, and Loving the Great Game of Life

Skip Johnson

1264 Old Alpharetta Rd.
Alpharetta, GA 30005

Although the author and publisher have made every effort to ensure that the information in this book was correct at the time of first publication, the author and publisher do not assume and hereby disclaim any liability to any party for any loss, damage, or disruption caused by errors or omissions, whether such errors or omissions result from negligence, accident, or any other cause.

All rights reserved. No part of this book may be reproduced or transmitted in any form or by any means, electronic or mechanical, including photocopying, recording, or any information storage and retrieval system, without permission in writing from the publisher. For more information, address Permissions Department, 1264 Old Alpharetta Rd., Alpharetta, GA 30005.

Copyright © 2013 by Skip Johnson

BookLogix paperback edition August 2013

ISBN: 978-1-61005-386-0
Library of Congress Control Number: 2013913244

(For information about special discounts for bulk purchases, please contact BookLogix Sales at sales@booklogix.com.)

10 9 8 7 6 5 4 3 2   0 7 2 5 1 3

Printed in the United States of America

∞ This paper meets the requirements of ANSI/NISO Z39.48-1992 (Permanence of Paper)

To my mentor in the life of belief and optimism—my father,

Gordon Edward Johnson III

"When you arise in the morning, think of what a precious privilege it is to be alive—to breathe, to think, to enjoy, to love."

– Marcus Aurelius, *Meditations*

Contents

Foreword		xi
Introduction		xiii
Chapter 1:	The Pilgrimage	1
Chapter 2:	Playing Field or Battleground—Choose Your Life's Venue	9
Chapter 3:	The Journey Up the Steeper Part of the Mountain	23
Chapter 4:	Coaches and Teachers Arrive—Right on Time	29
Chapter 5:	Obstacles to a Life of Gratitude	35
Chapter 6:	Speaking of Gratitude	43
Chapter 7:	Retirement: Gracefully Exiting the "People-Fixing" Business	49
Chapter 8:	When the Heat Gets Turned Up: Staying Grateful in Really Challenging Times	53
Chapter 9:	Gratitude in the Game of Leadership	61
Chapter 10:	Now the Test: Living One Grateful Day	69
Chapter 11:	The Never-Ending Path: Becoming a Master in Living the Grateful Life	81
Chapter 12:	The Choice	91
Bibliography		95
About the Author		99

Foreword

I have found gratitude and its enriched layers to be lessons for living a complete life. The gift of our lives is magnificent and full of wonder. The beauty of life gives us so much for which to be thankful. You are the perfect person to write about something this important, and I know your book will teach us many things.

A mentor of mine loved me enough to share this, and I pass this on to you knowing it will affirm your wonder of the human condition and the human spirit. My understanding of how life works increased tenfold when I absorbed these words and made them a part of me a long time ago.

He told me that when two people are touching, their souls overlap, soothing the fears of separation and aloneness and allowing them to share a softer spirit that connects them to the human thread of life. I was stunned as I pondered what he had said. Could human connections work this way, really? As I grew older I understood clearly the wisdom of his words.

I expanded my understanding of this concept as I came to realize that through heartfelt words, either spoken or written, we touch each other in similar ways. The human connection streams into us and allows the words to settle in the right places of the soul. If only with our eyes and ears, still we are touching, and that remains a powerful, transformative experience.

Some people believe that all they have to do is think of their love and gratitude and that will be enough. It is not, for humans need to express this love and receive its beauty in return to make the magic happen. Our protective armor melts away when we fall silent in the reverence of this connection. Humanness happens to both the giver and the receiver with the smallest gesture of love, kindness, and gratitude. A sincere, well-worded thank-you has no equal. To be grateful, and to express this gratitude, simply rocks the house for us all.

Thank you for sharing yourself and your wisdom. You will touch the world with your words, and souls will overlap because of you. And we are all mighty grateful for that.

Tom Butler
November 20, 2012
Douglasville, GA

Introduction

First of all, I want to share with you that *Grateful for Everything* won't teach you to be "glad" all the time, including when something just plain awful—or seemingly awful—happens.

It *will* offer lessons on how to take the hand that we have been dealt, develop steps to become grateful for the lessons to be learned, and begin to weave it all into a mosaic of life that resembles a great game to play, rather than a mire to be trudged through on a daily basis. When we diligently study, learn, and apply these skills of being grateful for everything, our day-to-day experience shifts from trying to stay one step ahead of problems to consistently trusting and appreciating life and all the lessons that are presented to us.

One who understands and practices this understanding that life has a much better plan than we could ever engineer could aptly be called a master in the art of gratitude, a person who has matured to a level of authentic, grateful presence. When we are around these rare people, we feel comforted, inspired, and encouraged about the path we are all on together. This book will help you become that kind of person.

There will always be choices and challenges that seem to be calling our names. Our tendency is to hope that those choices and challenges will somehow not find us. We attempt to hide from them in a cocoon of peace, quiet, and security. Choosing to be grateful can refine our view and give us that comfort and renewal in the way that a gentle wind provides us with real relief from a blistering heat.

Helen Keller reminded us, "Security is mostly a superstition. It does not exist in nature, nor do the children of men as a whole experience it. Avoiding danger is no safer in the long run than outright exposure. Life is either a daring adventure or nothing."[i] When we increasingly incorporate thankfulness into our lives, we realize that it is not only safe but enjoyable to come out of the cocoon and see the great adventures that are awaiting us. Our contentment then lies in the remarkable ability to be at peace with our own insecurity.

It is a fact that we will face varying degrees of adversity. From daily annoyances to catastrophic world events, none of us are immune to eventual hardship and heartache. Yet in the same way that the world rights itself after disasters, we can recalibrate and recover in a renewing way from our own heartaches and emotional distress. Gratitude can be the primary tool in rebuilding our lives in a more effective, sustainable, and beautiful way.

Having shivered in the icy grip of personal tragedy and having also basked in the warm sunlight of success, I intimately understand this: Gratitude for what matters most in life is the common thread of wisdom that runs between these two extremes.

We need not wait until a crisis to live with gratitude. We can embed that same thankfulness deeply in our souls so that we respond to each daily task in a lighter, more carefree way—life as a great game begins to emerge.

Let's now begin our quest toward being *Grateful for Everything*.

---

[i] Helen Keller, *The Open Door* (New York: Doubleday, 1957).

Chapter 1
The Pilgrimage

A story is told that many years ago in a faraway land there lived a wise, spiritual elder at the top of a mountain. A young pilgrim traveled up the mountain to learn the secret of life from this teacher, and when the pilgrim arrived, the teacher invited him in to have tea. The old teacher simply said to him, "Every single day, be thankful." The young man thought he understood; they talked a little more, and he went back to his town.

The young man did fairly well throughout the year. He felt as if he was being appreciative, and he often said thanks. But something was missing. So the next year, he traveled up the mountain once more. He knocked on the door, and the old man invited him in to have tea, again.

The pilgrim told the mentor his situation, and the wise elder looked at him very calmly and replied, "Be grateful for everything in your life. Be grateful for everything." So, the young man returned home and throughout the year, he increased his level of gratitude, unlike anything he had ever done before. Through challenges, through struggles, he was grateful. He soon felt as if he truly had achieved a significant goal in his life—one that was incredibly difficult to reach.

The young man then returned to the mountaintop to share his good news with the teacher. When the teacher opened the door, the pilgrim *entered and excitedly shared with him the wonderful gift that he felt he had been given. As they had their tea, the wise man gently put down his cup and said, "What you have learned will change your life forever. Being grateful for everything takes life to a new level, so that it now becomes more of a great game, rather than a painful, ongoing saga. You will find that challenges become useful parts of the competition and that difficult people are simply opponents presented to help you play your best. Life itself will begin to take on a new meaning. But, remember: The great game will continue only as long as you choose to let it continue."*

Upon hearing these words, the young man returned home with a peace that he had never before experienced. The great game had officially begun in his life...[1]

The pilgrim in this story could be me, or it could be you. There are times in our lives when we just *know* that the secret to handling life's difficulties is just around the corner—or just up the next mountain. Maybe it's trying harder. Maybe it's doing more. Maybe it's doing less. Maybe it's asking the right person or buying the right thing or hearing the right phrase at the right time.

But, learning to be fully grateful? How could this possibly be the cornerstone in building a life that portrays the spirit of a great game, instead of a dungeon of stress, heartache, and pain?

As we journey in this book, we will see how developing and using gratitude—especially during difficult times—can help take seemingly insurmountable complexities and transform them into gentle reminders that life's richness can many times be found amidst what often seems like life's rubble. We'll learn how gratefulness can be the alchemist that slowly, yet almost magically, transforms a gut-wrenching feeling of despair into the enlightened understanding that life is not only bearable but maybe even *wonderful*.

It's true that when times get tougher and tougher, we often think that we are at the point where we cannot take one more step. Yet even at that perceived breaking point, we can use the skill of being constantly appreciative, just as the pilgrim in our story was taught. We'll see the transcending, comforting power of being grateful—even then—and we'll experience how it is soon accompanied by peace and contentment, if we can only trust and press on.

As you proceed, keep in mind that whether your current stressful situation is related to a job, family, health, finances, or just all-around stress, as you get close to a greater understanding of the power of gratitude, you will actually appreciate what those "obstacles" bring you. You will begin seeing the role they play in your life's plan.

You may also find yourself subtly arguing that you have little to be thankful for, especially compared to others. How could you ever get to the stage that Nietzsche shared when he so confidently wrote, "My formula for greatness in a human being is *amor fati*: That one wants nothing to be different, not forward, not backward, not in all eternity…Not merely bear what is necessary…but love it."[2]

How can I get *there*? The answer is that we simply must begin. We must start down the path in a determined way and trust the journey to gratefulness to unfold for us as we press on. Failing to begin means we accept by default that life simply wants us to stay helplessly in our rut, waiting for a better day. There is an unexplainable, omnipotent power that is released in us when we gratefully embrace the unknown in our lives.

When we begin, we open the door to the same power that Ralph Waldo Emerson referred to when he said, "The measure of mental health is the disposition to find good everywhere."[3] *A measure of mental health!* As we choose to be grateful, as we choose to look for the good, we are solidifying and validating our positive mental health—how amazing!

It's a choice, yet often, we think it's not *our* choice. However, we'll find that when we make a decision in our lives to be grateful, even if it's for something as simple as gratefully getting out of bed one more day when we don't really want to, we are beginning to understand *amor fati*—the concept of living in such a way that we truly embrace life as it is. We are affirming elements of good in our lives. As we begin enumerating the many people, things, and experiences we have to be thankful for, the "snowball effect" happens. Situations *somehow* begin appearing brighter, and we become more hopeful.

Acknowledging what we have to be thankful for activates a chain of good that becomes undefeatable. Margo Barnard, an astute, compassionate, and highly-regarded Georgia psychotherapist, echoes this potential found in gratitude. "A very wise man once told me that there are two kinds of prayer: 'Give Me' and 'Thank You,'" she shared with me. "'Give Me' narrows the field of vision to disappointment and frustration. Each moment presents an opportunity for our consciously choosing a 'Thank You' prayer. This expression of gratitude allows space for seeking and noticing the gifts of this life—an easy task when life seems abundant, and a truly worthwhile endeavor when life feels especially difficult."

Yes, even if we are in difficult times, we must begin. Choosing to cross the line away from envy, resentment, bitterness, and anxiety, and to move to thankfulness, is truly the beginning—the beginning of an authentic, empowered, and expanded life.

Finally, before we proceed further on this endeavor, let's talk just for a moment about the elusive "h" word—happiness. We'll discuss this issue more in depth later, but first of all, I'd like to be clear, fellow pilgrims, that gratitude in itself will not make us happy.

Nothing can *make* us happy. However, let's look briefly at how gratitude does fit into our whole happiness search (because it does), since happiness is what most of us really want in life—or at least that's what we *think* we want.

If we peel the onion a little, maybe what we will see is that we want the *feelings* of happiness—feelings of joy, exuberance, and peace.

If our good feelings are dependent on something outside of us, we are in for a long, frustrating journey. We don't have control over these externals. Things will come up, people will hurt our feelings, accidents will happen, and "bad" things will appear in our lives. If our happiness could come from the *inside,* then maybe those feelings could be generated by embracing life as it is—no external adjustment necessary.

Through gratitude, we create those feelings of happiness ourselves instead of being dependent on something or someone else. We can make our decision to be happy and remain unperturbed as life continues on around us—it will anyway, whether we stay calm or go kicking and screaming!

Maybe, just maybe, we can get to the level of the person the brilliant author Florence Scovel Shinn wrote about when she said, "He is undisturbed by adverse appearances, knowing that *Infinite Intelligence* is protecting his interests and utilizing every situation to bring his good to pass."[4] Maybe we can set goals and allow life's annoyances to simply be accepted steps toward reaching that goal. Don't we all, in some way, want that freedom which comes from trusting in the ultimate outcome of our situations?

There is a great new world waiting for us out there. It can be found by developing our skills in looking through the lens of the gift of gratitude—and the whole process can truly become a great adventure. We can learn to set our course, and anything along the way is simply another marker in reaching our destination. Small changes can evolve our state of being into one that is dramatically more resilient to waves in the storms of life that sometimes furiously pound away at us.

Dr. David R. Hawkins, in his book *Power vs. Force: The Hidden Determinants of Human Behavior,* notes that this concept is called the Law of Sensitive Dependence on Initial Conditions: "This refers to the fact that an extremely minute variation over a course of time can have the effect of producing a profound change, much as a ship whose bearing is one degree off compass will eventually find itself hundreds of miles off course."[5] In a similar way, little by little, increases in gratitude shape our lives. We begin by making subtle changes, which will eventually lead to meaningful results. Every time we use gratitude through our actions or words, we plant a seed. The more of those seeds we plant, the more the fruit "miraculously" comes back to us at perfect times, in situations where we seem to need it the most.

One more point: As we go through this book, you will find me referring to the importance of "breathing" as you work through your gratitude practice. Suffice it to say there are hundreds of books on the methodology of correct breathing—and this is not one of those books. What I *will* say is that a relaxed mind and body will dramatically increase your ability to find gratitude in your world, and deep breathing can lead to a deeper feeling of relaxation.

Dr. Andrew Weil, in his audiobook *Breathing: The Master Key to Self Healing,* comments, "Of all the techniques I have investigated for reducing stress and increasing relaxation, it is breathwork that I have found is the most time-efficient, the most cost-efficient, and the one that most promotes increased wellness and optimal health." So, spend some time learning to breathe deeply. A few minutes a day will significantly improve your gratitude practice and allow you to more gratefully accept the gifts that are soon to be on your path.

Breathwork is a tool I cannot recommend highly enough. One of the books I suggest is Dr. Herbert Benson's *The Relaxation Response*. It is a simple and extremely effective explanation of the power and process of his proven technique for incorporating relaxation into your life.

Take a moment, breathe deeply, and express thankfulness. Be thankful for the country you live in. Be thankful for your life experiences. Be thankful for your ability to laugh and love. Be thankful for the books you read or for the fact that you *can* read. Simply express gratitude and notice how you feel. Just as the young pilgrim did in our story, let's continue the journey further up the mountain to a richer, more fulfilled, more exciting life.

---

[1] Adapted from an essay by Abbott Shibayama. Zenkei Shibayama, *A Flower Does Not Talk: Zen Essays* (North Clarendon, VT: Tuttle Publishing, 1971), 188–191.

[2] Friedrich Nietzsche, *Basic Writings of Nietzsche*, trans. Walter Kaufmann (New York: Modern Library, 2000).

[3] Ralph Waldo Emerson, *The Complete Works of Ralph Waldo Emerson* (Boston: Houghton Mifflin Company, 1904), 62.

[4] Florence Scovel Shinn, *The Wisdom of Florence Scovel Shinn* (New York: Fireside, 1989), 111.

[5] David R. Hawkins, *Power vs. Force: The Hidden Determinants of Human Behavior* (Carlsbad, CA: Hay House, 2012), 52.

Chapter 2
Playing Field or Battleground— Choose Your Life's Venue

Life's a great game that we all get to play,

Or life is a battle we fight every day;

Life sets the stage to live, laugh, and love,

Or wait for more problems to come from above;

Life gives us lessons to learn and embrace,

Or miserable times that we all have to face;

We'll look to each day with sadness and dread,

Or start a new game when we rise from the bed;

When walking the tightrope, we stay calm and trust,

Or think with resentment how life is unjust;

Life's a great game or a battle each day,

And we get to choose if we'll fight or we'll play.

As our expedition unfolds, we want to be clear on how we will view the context of our quest—and our overall lives—because there are two fundamentally different ways of looking at our world: life is either a great game and an adventure, or it is a daily battle and a grind. The way that we *choose* (we'll use that word a lot) to see it is incredibly important since it shapes our views on everything we do. For example, even in the "dog-eat-dog" business world, many CEOs are beginning to realize that fun and work are not necessarily incompatible—in fact, having fun can be an efficient way to do business.

John Sculley, former CEO of Apple, painted a very clear picture of this concept when he said, "People are going to be most creative and productive when they're doing something they're really interested in. So having fun isn't an outrageous idea at all. It's a very sensible one."[1] This is a far cry from the days of abrasive, intimidating leaders who believed that they could guilt or force their workers into doing more and better work. People are engaged and effective when they know that they and their work are valued. Whether the great game is played at home, at work, in the classroom, or whatever venue, there is the distinct feeling of connectivity, common vision, and commitment that tends to be present.

More and more success-minded individuals and groups are beginning to understand the effective concept of having fun at what they do. Each of us can look through those same filters. However, if you choose to see through other lenses, the world will accommodate that and give you plenty of evidence that your view is right. For example, you can feel a pure sense of despair. Mike Tyson's view of life had become one of a painful, never-ending battle when he said these words to a reporter at *USA Today* in 2005: "I'll never be happy. I believe I'll die alone. I would want it that way. I've been a loner all my life with my secrets and my pain. I'm really lost, but

I'm trying to find myself. I'm really a sad, pathetic case. My whole life has been a waste. I've been a failure. I just want to escape."[2]

Although there are times we will feel sad and there are times we will feel discouraged, our overall view of life's inherent goodness *is* a decision—one that we may freely choose. In the high-stress Western world, we often feel that we are simply dragged along by a current of anxiety and strain, and that we must fight our way out of our problems every single day. We hear comments like: "Better not slow down, there is someone right behind you," "Don't let up, someone is there to take your place as soon as you do," or "You'll have to claw your way to the top."

These clichés lock themselves into our subconscious until we feel that everywhere we look is another reason to pick up a figurative weapon and fight. Gratitude, on the other hand, tells us to trust that things are working according to a master plan and that there is plenty of room for success for everyone. Gratitude lends itself to the thinking that life really is a great game and a lot of fun if we will look through the filters of personal challenge and achievement, rather than beating our adversaries over the head and sprinting across the finish line as quickly as we can.

Baseball legend Derek Jeter knows the power of incorporating a "great game" mentality into your world. He offered, "You gotta have fun. Regardless of how you look at it, we're playing a game. It's a business, it's our job, but I don't think you can do well unless you're having fun."[3] You'll essentially see this in any athlete that plays at a sustainably high level. Watch great tennis players, golfers, martial artists, and others and you'll see that the elite performers have less force and more of a sense of play and relaxed power in their performances.

In case you're wondering, having fun does not equate to being silly. Having fun does not mean we don't care about what we do.

Having fun does not mean that we are irresponsible. It means that there is a joy, a carefreeness, and a trust that permeates our actions.

Developing this spirit of "the great game" doesn't mean that life will necessarily be easy (but it can definitely be easier!), and it doesn't mean we shouldn't diligently plan, set goals, and be disciplined in our efforts toward reaching them. But seeing life as a great game, we choose to find an element of fun in our activities and we begin to relax and uncover traits that can guide us toward our triumphs, and so life feels more like a swim with the current rather than an upstream struggle.

Instead of trying to control life, we can learn to gratefully let life flow through us and we'll soon begin seeing the fruits of our efforts as we gradually let go. Yet for some reason, we feel the need to clutch so tightly (often literally) and hope that we can just *survive* the battle we are facing. Maybe if we are willing to put down the weapon, take off our armor, unclench, and breathe deeply, we may see the battleground morph into an inviting field of play. Here are some traits that should manifest gradually in your life when you change your view, raise your level of gratitude, and see life as being a "great game":

Gentleness. Many often think of gentleness as being a trait of weakness. On the contrary, when we become gentle, life opens up to us and allows us to be creative. We connect with people, and we attract people into our lives who we normally may not, because gentleness in our demeanor actually seems to produce an element of irresistibility. A person who has learned the art of living in a gentle way develops a power that appears to be effortless. This impact of gentleness when incorporated in our lives is expressed in the following poem I wrote some time ago for my daughter Emily's high school graduation:

They Who Live Gently

The air fills with laughter and love when they're near,
And words that they choose have no mandate or fear;

Their strength comes from softness that's strong as pure steel,
And when in their presence, compassion is real;

They've been through the trials and the fires we must face,
Yet they understand that each has its place;

The tracks that they leave whenever they go
Are typically light, but impact you so;

They won't say their lifestyle is one that's deserving,
There's no time for that while they're loving and serving;

For most of us this way of life is but dreams,
Yet this way for them is so natural, it seems;

They won't boast their secret, but learn it you must:
Live gently, live bravely, live life built on trust.

The power of gentleness was beautifully affirmed by St. Francis de Sales when he said: "Nothing is so strong as gentleness; nothing so gentle as real strength."[4]

Patience. This is another characteristic that becomes more prominent as you add gratitude, and it's something that you will find indispensable as you continue on your gratitude path. Patience is defined as "bearing pains or trials calmly or without complaint," and South Carolina Governor Nikki Haley certainly personifies this trait. Gov. Haley, a daughter of Indian parents, recounted the time when, as a child, she and her sister were disqualified from a small-town South Carolina pageant because of their race.

"They pulled my parents aside and said they had a white queen and a black queen and they didn't want to upset either side by putting us in that category,"[5] she recalled. Later on, Haley, who authored the book *Can't is not an Option: My American Story*, graduated with an accounting degree from Clemson University. Then she entered the world of politics, after being inspired by a speech she heard Hillary Clinton make at Furman University. Haley remembers Clinton's message, "She said, 'There will always be people who say you *shouldn't* do something, but the only thing you should…think about is why you *should* do something.' She said, 'Don't listen to the naysayers.'"[6] Haley took heed of those words and *patiently* worked her way up the political chain and eventually became the state's first non-Caucasian governor.

You will find plenty of opportunities to practice patience, so instead of being annoyed, learn to relish those times as opportunities to successfully improve in this part of the great game.

Courage. You'll find that your courage will seem to rise as your thankfulness is elevated. Rudyard Kipling, in his poignant and inspiring poem "If," speaks to the heart of this as he addresses practical examples of situations where courage will be required from us daily. Look at his opening words:

If

If you can keep your head when all about you
Are losing theirs and blaming it on you;
If you can trust yourself when all men doubt you,
But make allowance for their doubting too:
If you can wait and not be tired by waiting,
Or, being lied about, don't deal in lies,
Or being hated don't give way to hating,
And yet don't look too good, nor talk too wise;

As we become more grateful, we will likely see a new or renewed sense of courage. This courage can trample many of our fears and propel us forward with a diminished concern for the safety of our ego, which we falsely believe will provide us security and peace. Each brave choice we make and each courageous action we take, we should privately and gratefully acknowledge as another useful victory in playing the great game of life.

Enthusiasm. It would be nearly impossible to grow in gratefulness and not grow in enthusiasm. In fact, you could argue that people's enthusiasm is typically proportional to the gratitude they have in their lives. As your appreciation for all that life brings you grows, you simply feel better about *you*. And when you feel better about you, you share that with others through an enthusiastic manner, which is nothing short of contagious.

Enthusiasm doesn't mean appearing excessively happy or extroverted. A person who is enthusiastic can often be soft spoken, but whether they are soft spoken or not, they radiate belief and they glow with genuine trust in an outcome. If one starts with the decision to be enthusiastic, then almost magically, people will gravitate toward that trait. You can almost feel the exhilaration and the "great game mindset" relating to enthusiasm in this quote by Dorothy Sarnoff, former speechwriter for some of the great orators, such as former president Jimmy Carter:

> Enthusiasm is the greatest business asset in the world: it beats money and power and influence. Single-handedly the enthusiast convinces and dominates. Enthusiasm spurns inaction. Like an avalanche it overwhelms and engulfs all obstacles in its path, sweeps aside prejudice and opposition, storms the citadel of its objective. Set the germ of enthusiasm afloat in your business: carry it in your attitude and manner; it spreads like a contagion and influences every fiber of your industry; it means joy and pleasure and satisfaction to your workers; it means life and virility; it means spontaneous bedrock results—the vital things that pay dividends.[1]

Enthusiasm can make changes where many believe that change would be impossible. It pulls everyone into "the great game" and immediately raises the pulse and energy of those around us who would otherwise glumly sit among the staleness of the pessimists. If there is one "magic bullet" that will almost guarantee a mood change of a person or group, it is the injection of enthusiasm into their environment. The more you practice being enthusiastic, the more easily and habitually enthusiasm will flow into your life. Look for any chance you get to throw some genuine enthusiasm into your interactions—you'll find that the results will quickly and pleasantly surprise you.

Encouragement. This is another characteristic that grows as gratitude grows. Encouraging others becomes possible in a grateful life because we begin trusting that our needs will be taken care of, and we rightfully believe that "there is enough to go around."

Encouragement is as much a manifestation of faith as anything I know of. "Goethe put it this way: 'Treat a man as he is, and he will remain as he is; treat a man as he can and should be, and he will become as he can and should be.'"[7] The challenge is often that we are afraid to begin encouraging others because we don't know how, or we don't feel worthy or successful enough to reach out to others. But the person living the grateful life knows that the power of encouragement is one that is available to all, so the most effective method is to just start.

As with your gratitude practice, even a little encouragement will produce great results, and it will then give you confidence to spread encouragement to all you see who have a need—which is pretty much all of us! The fascinating thing about genuinely complimenting other people is that it is such a rare activity, yet the results are loved by essentially everyone.

So those are some of the exciting improvements you'll see as you develop your gratitude muscles. Sometimes they will evolve slowly; sometimes they will appear quickly in words and demeanor. On the other hand, if you choose to retain a "battlefield" view of the world, here are some of the traits that you can expect to appear and stay in your life:

Stress and anxiety. Here are some sobering facts from the Anxiety and Depression Association of America website[8]. Did you know:

- Anxiety disorders make up the most common mental illness in the United States, affecting 40 million adults, ages 18 and older (18 percent of US population).
- Anxiety disorders also cost the United States more than $42 billion a year, almost one-third of the country's $148-billion total mental health bill, according to "The Economic Burden of Anxiety Disorders," a study commissioned by the ADAA (*The Journal of Clinical Psychiatry,* 60(7), July 1999).
- More than $22.84 billion of those costs are associated with the repeated use of health care services; people with anxiety disorders seek relief for symptoms that mimic physical illnesses.
- People with anxiety disorders are three to five times more likely to go to the doctor and six times more likely to be hospitalized for psychiatric disorders than those who do not suffer from anxiety disorders.

Seeing life as one battle after another sustains the feeling that there are more problems and enemies around the corner so "I'd better get ready for them." This causes more distress, thus perpetuating the anxiety cycle, and the battlefield becomes a consistent place of stress for you—and for those around you.

Conflict. When we lack gratitude and don't feel as if we'll "have enough," it puts us in direct conflict with those we feel have more than we have and also with those who have more than we think they should. Consequently, we are constantly looking for reasons not to trust others, not to allow others to get ahead of us, and not to engage in mutually beneficial dialogue. And the struggle goes on.

We have the potential in playing the great game each day to achieve both small and also potentially great victories, if we can just trust that things will work out as they should. However, if we are bound by a conflict mindset, we spend far too much time subtly scheming about how to make things work *our* way in *our* favor so we can keep ourselves propped up on our self-perceived pedestals. We will do virtually anything we can to "win" in the battle we feel that we need to fight for ourselves or our loved ones. Therefore we are never able to rest in the journey—we are always looking over our shoulder for the crumbs we may have dropped, or looking forward to the next big thing we might miss if we aren't supremely vigilant. We remain constant, stressed prisoners of the very spirit that we think will make us victorious.

Manipulation and control. In a similar way to conflict, living life as a battle makes us feel the need to get our way at almost any cost. If I am battling with you, then I had better figure out some way to win, and it doesn't necessarily have to be the traditional, ethical way. One of the many problems with believing this is that you end up losing trust with just about everyone in your life. Each person you have in your world becomes either someone who is out to manipulate and control you or is a potential target of your manipulation and control. Healthy, relaxed, and mutually-trusting relationships are nearly impossible in this type of environment.

Another problem, as we will see, is that control is really an illusion to keep us feeling safe and significant, and manipulation is a tool to further that end. Any type of interaction or relationship that is based on this premise is potentially toxic and likely doomed from the start.

Pessimism. If a person's world is a battleground, it's likely that pessimism is embedded somewhere, and it will continue to grow. It could be as subtle as constant, annoying complaining about anything that can or "will" go wrong, or it could be as insidious as regularly looking for ways to sabotage other people's lives.

The challenge in overcoming pessimism is that the more we think pessimistically, the more we speak in pessimistic terms, and then consequently the less optimistic we feel about our lives. This potential problem is summed up well by business executive Frank Outlaw who said, "Watch your thoughts; they become words. Watch your words; they become actions. Watch your actions; they become habits. Watch your habits; they become character. Watch your character; it becomes your destiny."[9]

The whole cycle begins with our thoughts; our speech then becomes consistent with that mindset. This negativity tends to perpetuate itself and make it rare that a person "on the battlefield" experiences fun, enthusiasm, or *joie de vivre*, since the pessimistic mindset tends to constantly look for (and find) what's "not right" in circumstances.

Gratitude thrives in an environment of challenge, fun, and trust. It wilts in the war zone of fear, tension, anger, and constant motive calculation. So, look back over these attributes and ask, "Which world do I most often live in and which would I *rather* live in? Which lenses would fit my glasses better?" Although all of us will likely find ourselves pulled onto the battlefield at times, I think you'll agree that the choices leading to seeing and living life as a great game are wiser decisions for ourselves and for those people who are a part of our daily walk.

---

[1] Bob Nelson, *1001 Ways to Reward Employees* (New York: Workman Publishing Company, 2005), 173.

[2] Jon Saraceno, "Tyson: 'My Whole Life has been a Waste,'" *USA Today*, June 02, 2005, 1B.

[3] Randy Howe, ed., *The Yankees Fanatic* (Guilford, CT: Lyons Press, 2007), 194.

[4] Saint Francis de Sales, BrainyQuote.com, Xplore, Inc., last modified 2013, http://www.brainyquote.com/quotes/quotes/s/saintfranc193305.html.

[5] Susan Page, "Don't Say 'No' to South Carolina Gov. Nikki Haley," *USA Today*, April 03, 2012, 1A.

[6] Ibid., 2A.

[7] Stephen R. Covey, *Principle-Centered Leadership* (New York: Fireside, 1992), 59.

[8] "Facts and Statistics," Anxiety and Depression Association of America, last modified November 2012, http://www.adaa.org/about-adaa/press-room/facts-statistics.

[9] "Watch Your Thoughts," Quote Investigator, last modified January 10, 2013, http://quoteinvestigator.com/2013/01/10/watch-your-thoughts.

Chapter 3
The Journey Up the Steeper Part of the Mountain

If we did all the things we are capable of doing, we would literally astound ourselves.

– Thomas Edison

In the early stages of your journey to the peak of gratitude, you'll notice something interesting that starts happening. You'll see the subtle transformation to focusing *outward* on the rewards of potential success, instead of inward on the penalties of possible failure.

You begin paradoxically feeling that you have more control over your life because you have *chosen* to essentially give up control. By doing so, you begin gradually trusting that things are going to work out okay—actually better than okay. There is this distinct, intuitive feeling that you can let go and count all of your "haves" instead of your "have nots."

Life becomes more of an experience of appreciation, instead of resentment. It slowly allows you to open up to the joys, small wins, richness of faith, and the peacefulness of a softened spirit. Gratitude allows us to be a part of the peace that comes from an acceptance and appreciation of the way life's current is flowing.

However, as on any path, potentially challenging digressions will appear. As Dr. Seuss said in his book *Oh, the Places You'll Go!*, "You will come to a place where the streets are not marked. Some windows are lighted. But mostly they are darked."[1] Fortunately, the beauty of the digressions and diverging paths is this: Each path has experiences for which to be grateful. *Therefore, you can't take the "wrong" path.* So, potential regrets can be converted into a trusting attitude of thankfulness if we will choose to do so.

Regardless of the path we take, we can realize useful life lessons and growth when we decide to genuinely accept that these lessons are leading us in a direction that we ultimately need to be led. Unfortunately, as human beings, we tend to second-guess our choices, doubt our intuition, distrust our own vision, and therefore spend much of our time and energy playing the "if only" game: "If only I had gone to this college." "If only I had married my high school sweetheart." "If only I had said something else on that day."

Gratitude dissolves the "if onlys" and replaces them with bigger-picture "thankfullys." We can then accept our decisions, forgive ourselves if it's needed, and be emotionally and psychologically freed up to make a worthy difference in our own world and in the worlds of people around us.

Will this take time and persistence? Yes, and there will be friends and foes both who will tell you that this mentality "won't work." Life is full of people who will tell us the grass is greener somewhere else, and we need to hurry up so we can get more, have more, and do more to get to the top...quickly!

Gratitude leads us to slow down, embrace our present situation, uncover the beauty of the moment, and gently work toward making life richer and more meaningful for ourselves and our community. It shows us that being supremely patient on our journey will allow us to find a measure of joy in the experiences laid out for us in our daily walk.

But, it's important to remember that it is a daily *walk,* not a sprint!

To take the next grateful step up the mountain, patiently notice throughout your day how the people, your surroundings, and your blessings actually all do fit so nicely together. Simple gratitude for each of these pieces of your current life will allow you to appreciate the preciousness of this stage and prepare you to trust that your next step will be just as it should be. The temptation will be to think that life needs to be some way other than it actually is, but as your newly-appointed gratitude mentor, I would again heartily advise you to avoid that type of thought process. For instance, this is what I often hear: "Once I get out of this place, or get rid of this person, or dump this plan, or move or retire…then *everything* is going to be fine." Well, here's the deal: It's *not* going to be "fine." It's not going to be fine because the people who think like this haven't decided realistically what "fine" really is.

If to them "fine" is when everything is going to be safe, problems disappear, and everything will be challenge-free…well, it won't be fine. The type of person who believes this way has not embraced the lesson that our wise elder pointed to—that to a great extent "fine" can be whatever is put in front of them. Fine is not necessarily "liking" something, but it is accepting the moment, dealing with it without resentment or anger, and—get this—being actually grateful for the lessons to be learned and for our increased ability to trust.

Now you might be thinking, "So I just sit back and watch, and I don't do *anything when I am dealing with significant problems in my life?*" Well, you can passively accept your situation—if that's your choice. But that is not what I'm suggesting to do here. The goal is to get to the point where you see that the reaction or response is *all your choice.* The power of acting this way lies in the fact that you are now choosing to accept the reality of your situation; then, you can choose to do something about it, one conscious step at a time. You will be more emotionally free to make decisions about whether to change or stay in your current situation.

This concept of consciously handling things "inch by inch" was reiterated by author Eckhart Tolle when he wrote, "Doing one thing at a time means to be total in what you do, to give it your complete attention. This is surrendered action—empowered action."[2] At first it will feel awkward and forced, but don't let that stop you. Your feelings will soon become different. When we fully immerse ourselves in the present, there is no time for past regret or fear of the future. But what do we typically do? We start weaving a long, dramatic tale about how awful or time-consuming it's going to be to go through our current issues and how there are so many other things we want to be doing or places we wish we were.

Pretty soon we are miserable, and we feel as if everything in our lives is going to fall apart forever—and all from looking at our experiences in an ineffective way.

Now, you might tell yourself that surrendered action may work on small issues, "but what about when it comes to standing up for issues that are really important to me?"

If this happens, continue to be patient, press on, and be grateful for the lessons you are learning. (Remember our pilgrim's continued struggle?) It may be a forced expression of gratitude at first, but maybe, just maybe, you will then see that it is simply your journey in gentleness and persistence. Maybe it is your "lesson to learn" to figure creatively how to handle this challenge, and if you can look at it as an opportunity to endure and mature, then one step at a time, the best solution will appear and your personal growth will go to a new level.

But as long as your attitude is resistant, the more your attitude ties "who you are" to the problem. It becomes your identity.

When those limitations become "who you are," you often tie in your resentment, your anger about the situation, and your frustration about that perceived problem. Then, pretty soon, you have fully connected that deficiency mindset with your value or worth—or lack of. It becomes difficult to escape that belief.

Let me remind you: It's important to realize that the things we are dealing with are simply things that are put in front of us. Nothing more, nothing less. And that is all they ever will be when we choose to see them that way.

To know that we will always have situations that are challenging is actually a freeing concept. It allows us to be aware and then minimize their impact as we put them in perspective and redefine them as only "the next thing" on our path to a fully empowered, grateful life.

---

[1] Dr. Seuss, *Oh, the Places You'll Go!* (New York: Random House, 1990).
[2] Eckhart Tolle, *Stillness Speaks* (Novato, CA: New World Library, 2003), 64.

Chapter 4

Coaches and Teachers Arrive— Right on Time

As you toss away your limited thinking, the teachers that have long been absent in your life will begin to appear and to guide you to miracles. But, remember, thinking that you must have limitations is like putting a barricade in front of you that will not permit those teachers to appear in your life.

– *Wayne Dyer,* Real Magic

All along the path of "life as a great game," we will find exactly the right guides that we will need for the trek. When we decide to see all of our life experiences and the people we come in contact with as coaches and mentors for growth, our gratitude for life goes to a different level. The moment we make the decision that our lives are simply coaching sessions and classrooms and that our daily activities are the lessons we're issued, we become grateful students. We begin thinking in terms of how our association or interaction with this person or that situation can allow us to receive valuable training that we never would have obtained any other way.

Unfortunately, for many people, life is seen as an evil instructor and the events of each day are viewed as unnecessary perils that have no connection to them or value whatsoever. Therefore, life becomes a monotonous continuation of happenings that are punctuated by occasional highlights and many useless, unwanted "problems" that never seem to end.

But to receive these lessons and to use them skillfully in our quest toward a more fulfilled and enriched existence, we must first be open to instruction and then start taking ownership of our lives as we use that new knowledge. There is no more room for the blame game in our lives. Steve Boozer, a wise barber in my hometown, summed it up quite well when he once told me, "I let my kids know that they're not ever going to be happy until they make the decision that they're in charge of their happiness."

In fact, maybe the only thing that keeps us stuck in the rut of being discontented is our decision to choose *discontentment*. Pema Chödrön in her book *Comfortable with Uncertainty* speaks to this concept of being dramatically influenced by our fearful, resistant thoughts as she teaches us, "Perhaps nothing ever really attacks us except our own confusion. Perhaps there is no solid obstacle except our own need to protect ourselves from being touched. Maybe the only enemy is that we didn't like the way reality is *now* and therefore wish it would go away fast."[1]

Being "grateful for everything" says that not only do we accept these events into our lives, but we also give thanks for the inherent good in them. By doing so, we gratefully accept the lessons involved, and we reach another level of contentment, wisdom, and insight. We learn the lessons from the game of life. But, the teachers and coaches aren't always obvious to us since they don't routinely take the form of our loving, first-grade mentor or our childhood volunteer soccer coach. In fact, some of our finest mentors aren't sent to us as guides to show us how to live but as guides for how *not* to live.

Several years ago, I entered a convenience store in Savannah, Georgia, and the milk deliveryman was sweeping the floor. He was carefully making sure that he erased all of his tracks and that he cleaned up any dirt whatsoever that he might have brought in with his delivery. After he left I commented to the clerk, "Wow, that guy really took care of his mess, huh?"

The clerk smiled and said, "I love that guy. He's great—always leaves the floor looking better than when he walked in! But, you know, you should see the mess the beer man leaves. Every time the guy walks out, the place is trashed. I can't wait to get him out!"

It made me wonder, "What kind of people are *we*? When we enter others' lives, do they look forward to seeing us because we lift their spirits and make their lives better? Or, do we wear our dirty shoes into their lives and set the example of what they *don't* want coming into their world?"

Once again, when we are thankful for the people we meet and for the places we go, that mindset is very quickly manifested in our presence, in how we treat people, and in how people see us. When we understand this concept and begin diligently seeking progress, our gratitude can evolve—it's significant to remember that it is not one-size-fits-all. For example, an incredibly advanced stage of gratitude would be exemplified by what Viktor Frankl discussed in his inspiring book *Man's Search for Meaning*. In this book, Frankl notes how life in the Nazi concentration camps was primarily an "every-man-for-himself" affair—with the exception of a number of inmates who bravely and graciously gave their last bit of food to fellow prisoners. He wrote, "We who lived in concentration camps can remember the men who walked through the huts comforting others, giving away their last piece of bread. They may have been few in number, but they offer sufficient proof that everything can be taken from a man but one thing: the last of the human freedoms—to choose one's attitude in any given set of circumstances, to choose one's own way."[2]

That is the zenith of the spirit of faith and gratitude. It is a spirit that is so trusting that it is willing to *choose* to give away necessities in a way that exudes love and appreciation and respect for life—it is teaching others in a way that won't be forgotten.

Now, the temptation is to say, "Oh, I could never do that. First of all, I'll never be in those kinds of awful conditions, and, secondly, I could never make myself be thankful for anything in a situation like that." Therein lies the problem. Gratitude is not about *being made* to do anything. In fact, gratitude is almost the antithesis of force. Gratitude does have power, indeed, but it is power through acceptance, gentleness, trust, adaptability, and love.

When you decide to make gratitude a high priority in your life, it will begin with simply making *choices* to be grateful. And one of those choices can be to thank your mentors, whether "positive" or "negative." You'll then start choosing to see through the illusion of good and bad, straight to the core of their instruction, which, as you peel back the layers and gently work your way through the background noise, will be quietly sitting there waiting for your attention and acceptance.

Sometimes the fruits of your labor will show up rather quickly, as Charlene Belitz and Meg Lundstrom refer to in *The Power of Flow*: "As you take these steps, you will find yourself moving into harmony, into oneness, into true aliveness. You'll be living life the way it is supposed to be: fun, light, purposeful, in concert with the rhythms of life."[3] Then again, sometimes the results will show up more slowly and subtly. However, as you increase your trust and allow your gratitude to flow, increasingly the guideposts and teachers will be there for you, if you simply look for them each day.

It's important to remember that even though our coaches in the game can point the way, it is up to us to make a decision to slow down and follow their guidance or move in the direction that they have shown us. But more often than not, how do you or I live each day? Hurried, frazzled, looking ahead? Possibly—maybe even probably.

The musical group Alabama sings about this modern-day predicament: "I'm in a hurry to get things done; I rush and rush till life's no fun. All I really got to do is live and die—I'm in a hurry and don't know why."[4]

If hurrying is your choice, so be it. The problem, however, is that more often than not, it's not a conscious choice to hurry. It's an unconscious race to get ahead, to get to the point in life where the "good stuff" is. Unfortunately, by looking ahead, we miss the markers that our mentors leave us about the *really* good stuff going on right now. Quite frankly, there's nothing much more sobering than the thought of getting to the end of life and realizing that we've been sold a bad bill of goods and that the greener grass has actually been right under our feet!

Look around. How many people did you or I "semi-interact" with today? How many people would have felt encouraged and appreciated by receiving five minutes of our undivided attention, yet we were so busy thinking about where we "needed" to be or what we just had to be doing, that we simply went through the motions of attentiveness and compassionate listening. Or how many opportunities and gifts did we leave on the table because we were so busy looking ahead to a payoff somewhere in the near future? The helpful instructors are all around, disguised brilliantly quite often, but nonetheless, they are there. It's time to gratefully acknowledge their presence, and the presents they bring us.

---

[1] Pema Chödrön, *Comfortable with Uncertainty: 108 Teachings on Cultivating Fearlessness and Compassion* (Boston: Shambhala Publications, 2003), 165.
[2] Viktor E. Frankl, *Man's Search for Meaning* (Boston: Beacon Press, 2006), 65–66.
[3] Charlene Belitz and Meg Lundstrom, *The Power of Flow: Practical Ways to Transform Your Life with Meaningful Coincidence* (New York: Three Rivers Press, 1998), xv.
[4] Alabama, "I'm In A Hurry (And Don't Know Why)," *American Pride*, 1992.

Chapter 5
Obstacles to a Life of Gratitude

Of course, we all prefer to grow through good feeling experiences more than bad feeling experiences, but unfortunately that's not how it works. Sometimes the most significant lessons come with significant pain, and so your ability to be with that pain and learn the lesson despite the itch to push it away is a key dynamic of growth. This is one of the ways in which there is no such thing as failure. Feeling like a failure can actually be a distraction from learning the lesson that will help you grow.

– Josef Shapiro

As we climb higher, there are obstacles to gratitude wherever we look…if we choose to see them. On the other hand, opportunities for gratitude abound wherever we look, too, if we choose to recognize them. I've entitled this chapter "Obstacles to a Life of Gratitude" because that's the mentality that many folks have. Frequently, if you listen closely, you will find that people are telling you by their actions or words, or both, "I can't really be grateful because…" and then proceed to offer a litany of reasons why life just isn't fair for them.

35

Well, we could spend a lot of time here discussing whether or not life is fair. However, we all have challenges—that is the reality for each of us in this world. It will serve none of us well to spend time worrying about whether or not fate has been more kind to me, to you, or to anyone else. If you tend to typically think of fairness from the perspective of who has the most "stuff," then you may want to remember that these outward symbols of happiness and prosperity are quite often the very symbols that keep us locked up in our own handcuffs.

If you or I spend more time thinking about how much we *do* have, then we will be amazed at the length of that list and how much we have been blessed with. A friend of mine once shared with me this idea: If you sat around a table with twelve of your best friends and each of you had to dump all of your "problems" on the table, you would most likely run home and count your blessings as soon as possible!

The perception of obstacles—or the perception of opportunities—seems to actually create self-fulfilling prophecies. For example, did you ever notice how people who constantly talk about how unfair life is appear to get more things to complain about as life goes on? It's seems to be a never-ending cycle. Yet, if we take away the "life is unfair" complaint then we start seeing how much *really is* fair in life. The obstacles seem to diminish and they appear to be transformed into useful stepping-stones on our journey.

On the other hand, when we continue to judge our success or self-worth by what others have versus what we have, we continue the unwinnable chase and tend to see ourselves as slighted. Then, our focus will continue to be—consciously and unconsciously—that we just don't have enough…and we never will.

But it's easy to justify our position as a victim. In fact, it's incredibly difficult to do otherwise. We often feel that we don't measure up, and we are led to believe that we are lacking. We are inundated by the media with the message to look and see how much we don't have!

So, we now want to learn to step out of this "reality" into a new reality, which is radically different. It's a reality that is fundamentally grounded in seeing what's working—what's right and what's acceptable.

It's a reality that says life is pretty darn good—if we will only see it that way.

We will likely see something encouraging begin when we choose to operate in this new realm. For instance, when we see potential scarcity or some type of threat, instead of reacting in a defensive way, we will more likely find ourselves softening and choosing words that support adherence to our new, optimistic reality. Then we may, in turn, find people responding to us in more accepting ways. We'll likely find ourselves embodying traits such as gentleness and kindness, as well as finding ourselves laughing more and encouraging those around us to do the same. We'll tend to find that obstacles are no longer catastrophic obstacles—they have miraculously and harmoniously faded away or been transformed into useful lessons for us on our path.

People who understand the power of living a grateful life have no need to get caught up in continually elaborating on their "problems," nor do they have a need to boast about their successes either, because their visions and rewards tend to come from a different place.

This was the case when I saw Jill Trenary, a figure skating world-champion, being interviewed more than twenty years ago after she had just completed an amazing performance in a major international competition. The reporter asked her if she had known the moment she successfully executed a triple axel that she had won the competition. Her comment was genuine and humble as she said, "I knew I had done my best and that was what was important to me." When our work—and our lives—come from a place of genuineness, gratitude is clearly present, and when gratitude prevails, it empowers the doer, and it resonates with others.

In addition to that type of heartfelt humility and sincerity, gratefulness gives us a noble strength that trumps so many disempowering emotions, including excessive fear. For instance, Bill Irwin was a hiker who completed the Appalachian Trail, which is one of the longest hiking trails in the United States, stretching over 2,000 miles from Georgia to Maine. Only 10 percent of the people who begin the quest are able to complete it, and Bill Irwin was one of the 10 percent—and he was *blind*.

Irwin, a recovering alcoholic who had previously smoked five packs of cigarettes a day, fell an estimated 4,000 to 5,000 times on rugged terrain and in icy rivers as he climbed toward his goal for nine months. It was all a great adventure and challenge for him, and as with many grateful achievers, his humility was evident when he quietly commented upon completing this awesome trek: "I'm no great example of anything. Any blind person that is capable could do the same thing if they wanted to go through the same difficulty."[1]

Although we may not be working toward winning world titles or climbing treacherous mountains, numerous other challenges will face us daily on our own paths. We'll encounter rude people, potentially frustrating situations, and scenarios that seem to be unbearable. We'll face backbiting colleagues, friends who betray our trust, and unforeseen difficulties. But the absolutely glorious part of all of this is: it's now exactly what we've been planning on and waiting for, and we will be ready.

As Nietzsche referred to in his doctrine of *amor fati*, this is our chance not just to bear life, but to love it! This is our chance not just to accept the complexities we face daily, but also to embrace them. And when we choose to embrace these "enemies," we have no enemies. So the choice becomes this: Do we choose to resist them, being resentful of the experiences we encounter, or do we choose to embrace them and see them as partners on our journey to gratitude?

Either way, surprisingly enough, is okay. The beauty of it is that if we follow the choice of acceptance with, "I am grateful…" then there is no poor choice—it's all part of the curriculum in the classroom of life. One path just takes a little longer to get to peace that the other. However we choose, the situation rights itself beautifully when covered with gratitude.

With that being said, I would like to offer some ideas on what may be an obstacle/potential ally that is a little tougher to distinguish and to address than others, and that is the issue of impulsively acting on anger. This is another one of those land mines that can quickly derail your gratitude journey, and it's one temptation that is constantly waiting to rear its ugly head.

Notice I didn't say don't be angry. I said don't *impulsively act* on it, and there is a significant difference. Plenty of times in your life, things will happen to make you angry—and that's not necessarily a problem. The problem is how you manifest and then deal with that anger. Harsh reactions tend to throw the "great game" out the window.

I can honestly say that in my life, I can count on one hand the times I lashed out in a harsh manner after being angry and had those situations turn out well. Oh, and in case you were wondering, even subtle, passive-aggressive reactions are included in this category.

As David Lieberman comments in *Make Peace With Anyone*, "Rolling your eyes, tapping your foot, and crossing your arms may offer a degree of satisfaction, but you'll pay for it later."[2] Being angry and then acting on that anger in a harsh or hostile way is almost always problematic. First, although you "got it out" and told that person "the way it is and the way it's going to be," you may feel better, but, shortly afterward, you realize that the price is yet to be paid. You've sown seeds of fear, resentment, disempowerment, and possibly of retaliation. Not helpful.

Secondly, being angry and "blowing the deal" through an impulsive outburst gives you no room for creativity—no room for looking at different ways to solve a problem. There's no room to look at ways to peacefully handle the issue and to experience great personal improvement from it. Anger is simply an attempt to abruptly end a situation—but again, we should realize it is ending the situation only for that moment.

Thirdly, an angry reaction does nothing to help make your life better. Each time you get extremely upset with someone and allow your words to go unbridled, the temptation is to simply make it worse and worse by getting angrier and angrier. Thus you are now clearly moving in the opposite direction of self-growth.

Well, the gratitude student knows that we don't *know* what the other person's situation is in life. We don't *know* what that person is dealing with. We don't *know*, most of the time, why that particular person did what he or she did. Instead of being angry and then reacting in a harsh way, look for the opportunity to understand why that person did what they did. No need to look for solutions—just explore. You may see things differently, and you may even find some ground for compromise.

Learn to breathe, relax, and be curious. But a word of caution: This will not be easy and you will likely find that progress seems to be slow. However, I urge you to continue to practice in this area because the emotional payoff is huge when you are successful. Dealing well with this one shows who the superstars in living and loving the great game really are!

One final point on this subject: We *think* that we have now obtained some kind of authority over that person when we react. The reality of it is that we just built a nice little wall between us and them—a wall that will be tricky to deconstruct. Who is it really hurting when we act on our anger? Well, them, maybe. But, most likely, you guessed it…us.

And it typically goes back to a state of egotism, insecurity, and fear. Why did we *really* get angry? If we peel back the proverbial onion again, if we peel back the emotion, we will find a great deal of our own personal insecurity and fear under it all. What if instead of being angry, we simply stopped, took some deep breaths, and allowed the situation to pass through us?

Yes, there is the risk that the other person may feel as if he or she "won." So what? *Remember that by giving up control, we have actually retained control.* So who "wins"? Well, the winner is in the eye of the beholder—and if you need a winner (and I would not recommend validating that need), you could argue that it would be you, by virtue of the fact that you *chose* your response, you superstar!

Just keep in mind, when you lose your temper, you lose any kind of mastery over a situation. And when you lose that situational mastery, you have lost a lot more than just that perceived control—and the well of gratitude and all of its benefits immediately dry up. Maintaining your gentle, patient spirit conversely builds strength and allows you to gain affirmation that you are heading in the direction of being fully calm in the midst of the storms.

So, no matter what your obstacle seems to be, remember that these are now opportunities for you to make progress on your worthy yet treacherous quest that you would not be able to make any other way. Each time you succeed at recognizing and unmasking a "well-disguised opportunity," congratulate yourself—then keep moving up the mountain, because there are more great adventures ahead!

---

[1] "Blind Hiker Finishes 8-Month Trek on Appalachian Trail," *The Washington Times*, November 22, 1991.
[2] David J. Lieberman, *Make Peace With Anyone: Breakthrough Strategies to Quickly End Any Conflict, Feud, or Estrangement* (New York: St. Martin's Griffin, 2003), 31.

Chapter 6
Speaking of Gratitude

Remember that "Help us grow this grass" is a far more effective sign than "Keep off the grass."

— *Norman Vincent Peale*

"I was just kidding." "Good grief, I didn't mean it." "My gosh, they're only words."

Ah, yes, words. As we continue on our pilgrimage toward a fully grateful life, one of the tools that will be critically important is our choice of vocabulary. The quickest way to express gratitude or discontentment is through speech. Unfortunately, we often talk so much that we tend to take our words for granted. Yet, the power of words is irrefutable and, as Florence Scovel Schinn writes, "Your word is your wand."[1]

Now, before you start to believe that this is some silly affirmation, think about it with me, because the ability that you and I have to bring situations to pass with our verbiage *is* almost magical. Words *are* like magic wands. If you take just one hour and use nothing but words of gratitude, you will start to see a shift in your thinking, in your feelings, in your surroundings, and then in your being. It is as close to a magic act as you could imagine.

The magic is not simple, however, and the challenge is that as soon as you begin this Herculean effort with words of gratitude, you'll almost certainly be hit with opportunities for gratitude growth. They'll appear as well-intentioned friends or acquaintances who want to share some words in the form of a few problems with you—often problems that can't be solved, but certainly "need" to be brought to your attention! Or, they'll appear as bad news on TV or on the radio, which you'll be tempted to immediately relay to someone else. They may appear as pessimistic words running through your mind, or as words that give voice to problems or bad situations coming up (or potentially coming up).They can appear as guilt, unhappiness, or discouragement that beg to be brought to light.

But as these come onto the scene, breathe slowly and deeply, then let the issues approach and pass by. Then you can quietly, gently compensate for their arrival by speaking your words of gratitude. It will feel strange at first. We are as conditioned as Pavlov's dogs to jump into the fray. We believe that since this is the way it has always been, this must be the way it's supposed to be, and we join the pity party or the verbal attack. But, persevere, my friend, because the rewards are most certainly worth the effort.

As you get more consistent with your new response and new vocabulary, you'll find a relaxed feeling, a confidence, and a patient, lighter attitude toward the "junk" that is thrown at you daily. I repeat, however, that your ability to stay on a peaceful mental and physical course on an ongoing basis will surely be tested as soon as you really decide to make significant progress in this game of words.

As we discussed, you'll want to welcome those challenges that the pessimistic, potentially energy-draining wordsmiths bring and say, "Game on!" See them as the kind mentors who have come to help you securely lock in the new skills you are so eagerly trying to learn.

Acknowledge their presence, accept the gifts, and keep going. As the tension and tendency to instinctively, negatively react begin knocking on your door, breathe in, breathe out, relax, smile, and be grateful. Call on and repeat the powerful words of the wise man in our story who advised, "Be grateful for everything in your life. Be grateful for everything."

Continue to speak gratefully soon after the perceived crisis passes, and you'll be surprised by how quickly you recover your optimistic outlook.

I cannot emphasize the importance of this step enough, so let me remind you: At the point when your "buttons are pushed" by the words or actions of others, don't fall off the boat and start spewing words that are not in your gratitude toolbox, as most folks do. Instead, hang on! Those who patiently wait to see the opportunity for real breakthrough will soon be rewarded with a renewed ability to: respond rather than react; feel peace rather than anxiety; and view the situation with clarity instead of confusion.

Relax, breathe, and be grateful. As soon as the storm has passed and the winds subside, take the time and effort to verbally create your own rainbow by speaking words of gratitude. You'll feel the amazing comfort zone that's created, as if the deal is sealed. Then each time another opportunity is presented, repeat the process. The ease and effectiveness will increase as you allow yourself to trust the process to unfold again and again. It's a great game to play, but you will find that it's a challenging game, for sure.

As you train yourself in this concept of creating and speaking words of optimism, appreciation, and encouragement—where there would typically be resentment, anger, or tension—the process becomes ingrained. You'll see helpful effects show up in almost every aspect of your life, from relationships to your physical health.

As you choose your new words, at first it may seem as if nothing is happening. But, be assured, the ground is being prepared. Your language is causing the soil to become fertile. Press on—especially now, press on because your goal is close!

Yet, after trying repeatedly, as our pilgrim did, you may feel that something is still sorely missing—you may even feel that you are at the bottom of the barrel. Well, be thankful because that's as low as you can go, so the only way is up! See how it works?

If your first thought is, "That's ridiculous. I could never use words of thankfulness while in the depths of despair," then it's okay. Stay there if you *choose*, but remember that your actions are establishing your limitations, and when you choose those limitations through thoughts, actions, or words, you own them—or they own you. Let me remind you that the idea is not to be thankful for "being in the depths of despair." The wisdom lies in learning to be appreciative for the lessons you learn from being in those depths. Keep going, even though your ego will resist at first. The core of your being will seem to resist at first. But at some point, your verbal choices will cause frustration and despair to slowly but habitually melt, and something *feels* different.

As you use more grateful words, your concern about results continues to diminish. Something inside you *really* changes, and—like the mythical phoenix rising out of the ashes—you realize a transformation. You *become* the optimistic, courageous change you want to see in the world, and it all stems from your word choices.

Are you willing to make the shift to speaking words of gratitude, accepting the vast possibilities, and allowing people and experiences to come into your world to permanently, wonderfully impact your life?

Realize now that your words truly are your wand, and if they are words of fear, despair, resentment, manipulation, limitation, jealousy, and cynicism, then those traits will be your reward. If your words are those of hope, faith, courage, love, optimism, thankfulness, and patience, then your life will begin, and continue, to reflect that. This takes determination and focus, but, again, the wonderful gift is that a fresh opportunity is awaiting you and me every day.

Start today by choosing your powerful words wisely, and the next thing you know you'll have people asking you, "Hey, how can I get a magic wand like *that*?"

---

[1] Florence Scovel Shinn, *Your Word is Your Wand* (Radford, VA: Wilder Publications, 2009), 6.

Chapter 7
Retirement: Gracefully Exiting the "People-Fixing" Business

Remember these emotional buttons we have that other people push are simply pointing out to us where we need to do some inner work.

– Judith Johnson, "Huffpost Healthy Living," January 9, 2012

Certain habits must be set aside as we fully engage ourselves in our pilgrimage to the top. One of those habits is the energy-draining activity of playing gatekeeper in the lives of others. In her book *Codependent No More*, Melody Beattie says, "The surest way to make ourselves crazy is to get involved in other people's business, and the quickest way to become sane and happy is to tend to our own affairs."[1] Profound words. Simple concept. Rarely, rarely done.

A hallmark of the thoroughly grateful soul is the full acceptance of people just as they are. No tweaking or fine-tuning necessary. No, "you should" or "you ought to" or "if I were you, I would" or, my personal favorite: "Well, I'm not trying to tell you what to do, but..." It seems innate in many of us to project our agendas and our beliefs onto others. We just *know* that we could make someone else's life "better." We just *know* that with our help, that person could really, really, be just right. We could really fix them...so, we try.

Sometimes we try subtly and then other times we just lay it out there on the table. But there is a price when we choose these routes—there is *always* a price. Especially when we feel that we won the battle, showed them who was boss, or put them in their place. We have once again simply purchased ourselves a one-way ticket to a potentially complex, long-term conflict. We may not realize it at that moment and we may not feel anything but gratification and redemption, but what did it *really* solve, what personal growth did we *really* achieve, and why did we really do it *that* way? And, by the way, how could an element of gratitude have helped foster a different result in dealing with our tendencies to "fix" people?

First, let's remember that when we are playing the great game, it's not our "opponents" that cause us problems. No, the problem isn't what someone did or how he or she made you feel. The problem is, uh, you.

"Hmmm," you say. "You're sadly mistaken. You don't know what it's like dealing with some of the sickening, backstabbing, lowlifes I have to deal with." Yes, I would agree, I don't know. What I do know, though, is this: People who arrive in your life are only given authority to affect you, for good or for bad, if you grant them that authority. I also know that when we choose to focus solely on our personal improvement and on our contribution to the situation, it transforms the role these people play in our lives, so be grateful for each of them.

Once we make the decision to be responsible and grateful for these people being in our lives, we move to the next step: sharing the gratitude. In fact, share gratitude to the very person you feel like trying to fix! Now that we have learned the power of using words of gratitude, find something to thank them for about themselves—but it must be sincere, otherwise you have crossed the line into manipulation.

For example, you may hear people say that an effective way to change someone's behavior is to insincerely praise them or their actions. Well, first of all, it just plain doesn't work. I mean, you may feel as if you scored some quick points, but after your "compliment" is done, you're left with the residue of a lie.

Also, there is no compassion, love, or vulnerability in your gesture, so it's just hollow—it's an insincere attempt at fixing something or having a person like you. This caretaking takes absolutely no creativity or courage, and it provides no useful skill improvement in the way you play the great game.

Now let's talk about the alternative: genuine, heartfelt appreciation for someone or something. There is power in expressing sincere appreciation and gratitude—power for the giver and power for the receiver. A genuine gift of gratitude is close to the opposite of "fixing" someone. It's saying, "Not only do I accept you, I honor you."

But what if you might not feel ready to honor or express appreciation to the person that you feel needs fixing? No problem. Express it to someone else, *about* that person you want to fix. It's a close second in the "feel-good" category, and by being one level removed, it's easier. Many of the benefits are still there, and you are relinquishing your temptation to control.

Not quite ready for that? Then try expressing gratitude to anyone about anything. It works. It puts you in the mindset of embracing reality rather than fighting what you perceive as wrong. It focuses you on what's good, what's right, what's working, and what's just fine as it is. What you will find is that fewer and fewer people, situations, or things need to be fixed. You will have less energy focused in the wrong place and, consequently, you'll feel happier. Presto! Your retirement from the people-fixing business is complete and successful, so congratulations!

However, there is one more potential challenge. Once you officially retire you will have many opportunities to enter back into the people-fixing business, even on a part-time or occasional basis. You will have people who regularly appear on the scene who just generally seem to need to be "fixed" once and for all—or at least tinkered with a bit.

Don't do it! The cost will outweigh the benefit, and your comfortable retirement will turn into an ugly battlefield that lends itself to more conflict and angst. You will quickly rationalize that your help is desperately needed, and there is just no way that this person can make it through his or her situation, or life, without your personal, proven workmanship.

I would suggest that you ignore the enticement to re-enter the people-fixing field and staunchly stick to your exit strategy. In fact, here is a little rule to follow: When you see something that you don't approve of in a person, or when you hear them say something that irritates you, ask yourself, "Why? Why is this annoying me, and why do I feel the need to correct their behavior?" Chances are if you dig through a level or two, the answer will again be: "Because it reminds me of what I don't like about…me." Welcome to the world of responsible, personal growth.

So take some time and dissect the situation. Understand what it is that this person can bring of value to you. Your life is simply an ongoing compilation of experiences and interactions with various people, and the more you understand how these people can help you grow, the easier it will be to allow them simply to be who they are—without any of your potential "improvements." Now relax, enjoy your retirement—and let's continue on with our journey!

---

[1] Melody Beattie, *Codependent No More* (Center City, MN: Hazelden, 1992), 113.

Chapter 8

When the Heat Gets Turned Up: Staying Grateful in Really Challenging Times

I've missed more than 9,000 shots in my career. I've lost almost 300 games. Twenty-six times, I've been trusted to take the game-winning shot and missed. I've failed over and over and over again in my life. And that is why I succeed.

– *Michael Jordan, professional basketball player*

Like our pilgrim in the earlier story, we have burning questions that nag us as we continue toward the finish line in the great game of life. For example, let's talk for a moment about a subject that I'm sure even the spiritual pilgrim wondered: "How do I hold onto this gratitude during really tough times?"

Let's lay the foundation for answering that question by starting with another question: What would you say if asked what it is that you really want in life? You might say, "Just peace and bliss—that's what I would call a life of happiness. I'd like everyone to get along and not get upset.

And, ideally, I don't want anyone to act differently than I think they should—and then I would be happy."

If that's what you believe, then, unfortunately, as you may have found, the reality is quite different. Because people aren't going to do what you want, and they *are* going to do things that could disappoint and frustrate you and make your life challenging, but mostly *not* because of the reasons you might think. The reason you aren't "happy" in these tough circumstances is not that they are doing these things to upset your applecart; it's that you are not using your skills to deal with them. So, what's the answer?

Well, again, we accept that people are the way they are, and remember it's not our job to change them one bit—they are going to be the way they intend to be whether they get your approval or not (as we discussed in our previous chapter). Then, realizing that we can't change people, here's what we do—we don't fight it. Because the more we resist and wish things were different and the more frustrated and angry we become, the more we are setting ourselves up for disappointment.

Now, note the distinction: I said that *we are setting ourselves up* for these feelings to come in and embed themselves in our lives. I didn't say that anyone caused it to happen. We now clearly know that we have the control to decide whether or not we let these people interfere with our success, joy, or inner peace in playing the game. Because if you have someone who causes you pain and that person goes away, there will simply be a new "teacher" to come and teach you the lesson that you didn't learn before—the lesson that you are in control of your response. We can become people whose contentment is not dependent on anyone but us!

Getting to the point where we see that everyone—and every situation—is spectacular is a part of spiritual practice and the great game of gratitude and growth! Annoying coworker? "I'm grateful." Frustrating boss? "I'm grateful." Imperfect circumstances? "I'm grateful."

Remember, it's a subtle distinction: you aren't thankful for the problem itself, but for the lessons brought to you. You simply get to the point that there is no person, experience, or situation that can take away your values or peace of mind and sway your commitment to a great, grateful life. As we talked about before, you breathe in and breathe out, and then say to yourself, "I'm grateful." It's affirming that you are consciously moving forward in your journey—regardless of that person or what they are doing.

Anything that person or situation might bring to your life becomes background noise—or background music, if you will. When your entire being is focused on calmly breathing and being thankful, these external annoyances simply come into your life, float in a sea of calmness, and then blend in with the other thousands of stimuli you encounter throughout your day. They just become one more thing that affects you merely on the surface—and, at some point, not even there—because you reach the point where you are so unshakeable that the depths of who you are seldom change as a result of external factors.

The reality is that things are going to happen—"good" and "bad"—whether you choose to accept them or not. The only concern is how much pain the situation is going to cause you. How much energy, anxiety, fear, resentment, and resistance will you give it—or will you accept it, be grateful, breathe through it, and move on to the next learning experience in your life. Eventually, when you do accept all situations and become grateful through the problem or the challenge or the person that is causing your pain, and you quietly breathe through the situation, the obstacles simply become part of your peaceful landscape. You are left with your immovable attributes that no one or nothing can change…unless you consciously choose to allow that to happen.

Let me share a story with you about someone who has learned to brilliantly deal with difficult situations and make them simply "the next thing to handle": Richard Pawlowski is the maintenance manager at one of our family-owned health clubs in Atlanta. Richard has been with the company more than twelve years at the writing of this book, and he is one of the most dependable staff members we have ever had in the business.

Before this job, Richard had a job as a newspaper carrier. Every day, he would arise at midnight and begin his route at two a.m. Richard never missed a day/night of work—he just did not do that. In his new position in the health club business, his role was to be at the gym at four thirty a.m. to clean and then open the business for the start of a new day.

Richard lives about thirty minutes from the business so he would drive in each morning, get there a few minutes early, and begin his shift. One particular early morning, it was raining quite hard and Richard's car began sputtering on the way to the gym. As he pulled over, the car died. As Richard got out to see what the problem was, he stepped down strangely and twisted his right ankle quite severely. *Hmmm*…this was not good. Raining, three miles from the gym, less than one hour before a scheduled opening, with a twisted ankle. No, this was not good at all.

Did Richard call and say, "I can't make it today?" Did he sit in his car and wait until someone would hopefully come by to help? No, he put on his car flashers, closed the door, and began carefully walking toward the business—in a driving rain.

At five minutes before five a.m., he reached his destination and clocked in for his shift. Wet, wounded, exhausted, and deeply proud, as he should be, Richard Pawlowski was reporting—on time as usual—for duty.

For Richard, it wasn't particularly a choice. He *knew* that he was going to get there. He *knew* that he would make sure that no one had to worry about the maintenance manager fulfilling his promise to make his part of the operation successful, every single day.

In fact, he had chosen to conduct himself that way for so long that when it became extremely challenging, the decision had already been made to choose in a way that almost required no choosing. It was just the next thing that needed to be done to reflect his commitment and gratitude for his work, and so it was done.

Going to the next level during unusually difficult times may also mean that you aren't going to have your actions acknowledged publicly, but that doesn't mean those actions aren't equally important—and they possibly take even more courage than a publicly-appreciated action. I taught a college Sunday school class for many years and one young man in the class was beloved by all. His name was Ryan Stanger, and Ryan had an amazing gift for making other people feel special. Someone came up to me years after Ryan left college and told me a story. He started it by saying, "I know you know Ryan Stanger, and I want to share with you how Ryan changed my life from an act of courage."

Of course I wanted to hear about it because I had the utmost respect for Ryan, and I had heard many stories about his selflessness. "Well," the young man said, "I was a freshman in high school and was attending a Christian youth meeting called Fellowship of Christian Athletes (FCA). I was extremely shy in high school, and I was especially shy about attending my first club meeting. Along with a fairly large gathering of people, I went to sit on the bleachers in the gym as the meeting got started that morning before school. As the speaker got up to speak, I must have shifted my weight to get more comfortable on the bleachers and a large amount of change fell out of my pockets, down through the bleachers, and onto the gym floor. I literally wanted to crawl in a hole and die as all the attendees looked back in my direction to see where the incredibly annoying distraction had come from.

"Ryan Stanger, who was an upperclassman and the president of FCA, happened to be sitting almost right beside me at the time. Without hesitation, Ryan leapt to his feet in front of everyone and said loudly, 'Man, am I embarrassed! I dropped my coins all over the floor in front of *everybody*!' There was a deafening pause, and then everyone looked at Ryan and nonchalantly laughed it off. He had taken the fall for *me—and he barely even knew me!*

"Ryan proceeded to ask the speaker to carry on, and the meeting continued without a hitch, with no one even giving my traumatic event a second thought. But for me, it was a watershed moment. It showed me the rare power of someone who truly was secure enough, that trusted the outcome so much, that he could gratefully, even happily, take on my potential humiliation. It made me want to do anything I possibly could to give someone else that same gift. I personally understood and empathized with people who, as underdogs, had their security and self-worth almost snatched away, only to be rescued at the last moment by someone who had made a courageous decision to not let that happen."

As habitual gratitude takes hold in our lives, we find ourselves gradually filled with abilities and potential that never seemed available to us. We have the courage, the pride, and the belief that life is going to be okay—more than okay—so we can carry on with our duties in a way that turns our work and our work ethic into something that is truly special, empowering to others, and self-actualizing. Here are some words to focus on when you feel times are so tough that you don't know how to keep moving forward:

Keep Going

If they tell you you're beaten, don't listen;

If they tell you it's over, keep striving;

If they tell you you're finished,

Take a break, get replenished,

Then roll up your sleeves and keep driving.

For it's easy to quit when you're down,

It's common to give up—and most do;

But when you've persevered

After critics have jeered,

The one who's the winner is you.

So, when the heat gets turned up, let's understand that our happiness, even then, is truly in our hands. It's going to be tempting to think that the uncooperative co-worker or the unappreciative boss or the disappointing friend holds us hostage to their actions and antics—but they don't. Each time we choose to see ourselves as masters of our fate, life responds with a soft, encouraging whisper of, "You're getting there, my friend, you're getting there…"

Chapter 9

Gratitude in the Game of Leadership

A leader is best when people barely know that he exists, not so good when people obey and acclaim him, worst when they despise him. Fail to honor people, they fail to honor you. But of a good leader, who talks little, when his work is done, his aims fulfilled, they will all say, 'We did this ourselves.'

– *Lao Tzu*, Tao Te Ching

One of my favorite people is a woman named Juanita Clay. Juanita lives in Douglasville, Georgia, and she is the closest thing I have seen to a living Mother Teresa of Calcutta. Juanita runs a non-profit organization she started called A Gift of Love. Through this organization, Juanita provides a soup kitchen for underprivileged adults in our county and back-to-school supplies for hundreds of children each year. A Gift of Love also serves nearly a thousand meals at Christmas time to those who would go without otherwise. My daughters and I have been able to be a part of their activities over the years, and we all realize that this woman is truly special.

What makes Juanita unique is not necessarily what you would think. Naturally, what comes to mind is that Juanita is among the small minority in life who have dedicated themselves to really making a difference—and she does that. But Juanita takes service to a different level. She actually seems to *be* part of the groups and individuals she serves. In fact, as you watch Juanita interact with the children and adults she is giving to, she actually is one of them. She takes on their joys, their sadness, and their fears so compassionately that there is no visible distinction between the benefactor and the beneficiary. Juanita is an example of how, when we take on a life of high-level gratitude, we assume a sort of leadership responsibility by virtue of the fact that our lives will begin influencing the lives of others.

We never know where the ripple effect of our encouraging gestures will end. What we can be assured of is that anytime we do something as simple as writing an encouraging note or sharing words of compassion or offering our undivided attention to a person in need, the benefits will immediately begin.

Juanita Clay understands that real leadership comes with a responsibility that few will accept: the deep responsibility of leading with an element of service. It's a responsibility of putting others' hurts, pains, agonies, and worries on par with her own, and it's far from easy because Juanita surely must have her own laundry list of challenges.

Yet, by making a conscious decision to focus on the needs of others, the joy of gratitude takes over. And when gratitude takes over, there is no room for ego to reign. When ego is held at bay, we are also freed emotionally and mentally to empower others in a way that borders on being miraculous. Life takes on a whole new look.

All of us on the pilgrimage to gratitude will reach some type of leadership stage, and we certainly want to prepare ourselves as well as we can to live an empowering life that impacts others. But even for leaders—maybe *especially* for leaders—letting go is one of the biggest challenges that we face on the journey. Typically, we want to hold on tightly to our limited view of what's best for us and others. So, we spend most of our waking hours fighting to maintain the status quo when a richer life is right around the corner that exceeds anything we could personally construct, if we will simply trust the outcome.

In *The Power of Losing Control*, Joe Caruso writes: "Again, it's important to emphasize that any attempt to control anything other than oneself is always driven by fear—the fear that if we lose control even for a minute, something bad is sure to happen."[1] By expressing our thankfulness for our current situation, we let go of how we think things should be and gratefully accept the reality of how things are; then we're freed up to make more leadership decisions with more impact.

Generally, we think that we must force things to happen—we just *have* to do it and we have to do it *our* way. But maybe we can break that cycle by letting the situation unfold and allow for an even better outcome than we could have possibly imagined when we were "in charge." When leading is done through trust, confidence appears and people will connect with that. It can be so difficult, and frightening, to try and grasp the concept that, paradoxically, by gratefully giving up control, we gain control. When we do, that act can simply, lovingly guide our lives and help us lead others in a way that we previously couldn't anticipate.

Trusting that life is happening "right on time" is something that will allow us to feel a new degree of freedom—if we will only do it. Stop now and try it for just one moment…just trust, and notice how relaxed you feel.

I spent a weekend at a beautiful monastery just outside of Atlanta years ago. I remember talking to a monk who was clearly a grateful leader in his order there, a man who was also physically deformed. He was bent over and never could quite stand erect, but he was one of the most content people I have met. Apparently, he had been involved in helping to build the monastery years before and had been injured during the construction by a falling log that broke his back.

"It must be very painful," I said to him. He simply smiled and commented, "I have had, and continue to have, a wonderful life. I wouldn't change a thing."

He wouldn't change a thing? Incredible. In a very real way, this amazing man, this humble monk, knew a leadership secret that I wouldn't learn for many years: that by being genuinely, openly grateful in the midst of life's challenges, life becomes a challenge worth living gratefully for. And it inspires other people to rise to their own challenges. By giving up our desires for comfort, convenience, and ease, we open a new door, and we model a life of fulfillment and empowerment that causes our former desires and beliefs to pale in comparison.

The most successful, long-term leaders understand this concept. They understand that humbly, thankfully accepting the realities of life not only changes their world in a powerful way, but also changes the world of people around them in an equally powerful way. Ronald Reagan's generous, uplifting way of living, for example, had that effect on the people who were in his presence. When Peter Robinson landed a position as a young presidential speechwriter fresh out of college, he saw firsthand the impact that President Reagan's life had on those around him: "The longer I studied Ronald Reagan, the more lessons I learned," he said. "Instead of trying to remake human nature, as, for example, Lenin and Hitler did, Reagan simply told jokes—told jokes then threw back his head and laughed. We're all in this predicament together, the twinkle in his eyes seemed to say, but it'll come out all right in the end."[2]

That's exactly it. Gratitude for life, for the challenges, and for those around us gives us the faith and confidence to know not only that it will all be okay, but that we can help others see the same thing. It's a manifestation of the mentality of seeing life as the great game!

President George Bush, Sr., also understood the responsibility and privilege that this kind of leadership brings. He wrote, "For we are given power not to advance our own purposes, nor to make a great show in the world, nor a name. There is but one just use of power and it is to serve people."[3]

Leaders who embody this are able to lead in a way that is unique. Leaders who have evolved to lead with a generous spirit exude a credibility that is magnetic. It implores workers to move forward, to give more, to reach for levels that are inspirational to anyone nearby. Generous, appreciative leadership is contagious, and there is no need for credit because excellence has indeed become its own reward.

Dag Hammarskjöld, dedicated former Secretary-General of the United Nations, clearly understood this concept. He wrote, "Be grateful as your deeds become less and less associated with your name, as your feet ever more lightly tread the earth."[4]

Regardless of how it is manifested, gratitude is woven into the lives of most successful leaders, and it is typically of utmost importance to them. For example, Paul Lubbers, my good friend and director of coaching education at the United States Tennis Association (USTA), recently shared these words with me: "I am grateful for the opportunity to serve the tennis community—in my case to support the mission of USTA Player Development of developing top 100 players in the world. I am extremely grateful that in my work I am able to support the best coaches and players in the United States to help them reach their potential in both life and tennis."

The brilliant and successful secretary of state during the Bush administration, Condoleezza Rice, constantly shows gratefulness in what she does. "I'm quite convinced that a lot of my success has been because I was doing something I loved to do,"[5] she once said with a smile. On the surface, the comment seemed a cliché attempt at humility. Yet if you study the life and works of Rice, it becomes apparent that her comment is a real testimony to her faith in the unfolding of life—almost a credo. As a child growing up during the turbulent times of Alabama's civil unrest, Rice rose against extreme odds to hold one of the world's most powerful positions. Despite the evil around her, Rice's gentle determination and unwavering vision gave her the grateful belief that she was meant to make a difference.

This type of leader is rare, whether in a community or at the national or international level. But when gratitude is present in a leader's life, this one trait tends to transcend the other characteristics. Gratefulness is a manifestation of trust, and leaders with this type of spirit seem to be able to overcome seemingly insurmountable opposition in an almost effortless manner. Thankfulness acts as a ship's rudder, steering a leader toward the people, experiences, and places that tend to absorb and, in turn, communicate that energy in a wonderfully contagious way.

Jeffrey Gitomer, one of the most sought-after sales experts, understands the power of choosing gratitude in his daily work. Gitomer, who speaks to thousands of people each year, never seems to lose his enthusiasm on stage. Watching him work, you realize that this industry leader truly understands the gifts he has been given in writing and speaking, gifts that allow him to share his message all over the world. Gitomer commented to me:

> Grateful and gratefulness is a beginning, a middle, and an end. It's both a feeling and an expression. Be grateful for the skills you need or the opportunity you have as you begin any task or goal. Be gratified, proud, and grateful once a goal is achieved, and express your gratefulness to others who help or support you along the way.

It's important to note that being grateful must be felt on the inside first, or it can never be fully and sincerely expressed to others. Mike Alpert, beloved leader of the Claremont Club in California, who incorporates gratitude into every aspect of his daily life, shared with me:

I wake up every day and thank the Lord for all the opportunities and successes He has afforded me. I pray that I will be able to serve Him and do His will. I am grateful for being in a position to help others in need through my work. And, of course, every day that I see my wife and my daughter I am grateful beyond words. And I am grateful that I had the parents and grandparents who gave me love and direction.

If you are blessed with the opportunity to be in a leadership position, remember that gratitude is a trait that stands above many others, and it compensates for many skills that we might not have. Living and leading gratefully is contagious and will positively impact those you lead in a way that you could never imagine.

---

[1] Joe Caruso, *The Power of Losing Control: Finding Strength, Meaning, and Happiness in an Out-of-Control World* (Grosse Ile, MI: Brookshire Press, 2003), 111.

[2] Peter Robinson, *How Ronald Reagan Changed My Life* (New York: Harper Perennial, 2004), 155.

[3] George Bush, Sr., "Inaugural Address," January 20, 1989, http://www.britannica.com/presidents/article-9116858.

[4] Dag Hammarskjöld, *Markings* (New York: Ballantine Books, 1985), 125.

[5] "Condoleezza Rice's *Master Class* Quotes," Harpo, Inc., last modified February 13, 2011, http://www.oprah.com/own-master-class/Condoleezza-Rices-Master-Class-Quotes.

Chapter 10

Now the Test: Living One Grateful Day

So often times it happens that we live our life in chains. And we never even know we have the key.

— *"Already Gone," Jack Tempchin and Bob Stradlund*

The pinnacle of the grateful life is in your sight. Now the challenge really begins—and you're ready. What if, for one full day from sunrise to sunset, you could live your everyday life exactly the way that you want to live it? You could be exactly the person that you want to be.

Now, you can't change your circumstances in this hypothetical world, because you really don't need to change the world around you or your circumstances. Remember, you just need to change *you*. Because when you change you, then the world around you does the changing for you. So, what if you can be that person that you want to be for one day. How will you feel?

Well, I will suggest to you how you will feel. You will feel…empowered, gratified, content, and strong. You will feel alive. And what if you could take that day and do the same thing for two days, then seven days—one full week. Then what if you lived that way for a full month—fulfilled and content. Grateful. Loving the challenge of the game. You would feel an independence and a self-confidence which would be the springboard to a different level of life.

Now you can do the same thing for six months and then one year. Imagine yourself being the person you want to be for twelve straight months. The beauty of it is that it is all within our ability. We might think that our success in this endeavor is dependent on other people—our friends, coworkers, or family members—on everyone cooperating and playing their roles as we want them to play. But as we have discussed, the truth is that how well we do is up to us.

In fact, you could use this day to resist blaming anything on anyone. You'd be surprised at how difficult it is and you would notice how tempting it is to become defensive or to avoid taking responsibility for your actions. Our egos scream for significance! But, at the end of that *one* day, if we have chosen to take responsibility and to realize that this great, grateful day is waiting for us, then a tremendous feeling of freedom would come along with that realization. We would comprehend that this power is available to us in a lifelong way.

How would you live? How would your first day be spent?

Well, to prepare, it might help to start by thinking about what we *wouldn't* want versus what we *would* want. If we wouldn't want anger, we would choose to be peaceful all day. "Oh but that's too hard," you might say. Well, it may be hard, but so what? We're talking about only one day—and you can do just about *anything* for one day.

What if you wouldn't want frustration? Then you would simply be patient. What if you wouldn't want to be fearful? Then you would simply choose courage. The greatest news of all is that our determination to change, our "clearing the slate," is all in our hands—it's up to us! It's not controlled by an unappreciative spouse or dishonest politicians or the unfriendly clerk at the grocery store. It's a spectacular challenge and opportunity!

We would start out the day with a determination that life would be fundamentally good, regardless of what happens, and we would have a deep trust that everything is going to work out for the best. We'd have an acceptance and appreciation for everything that comes into our lives. We'd have an intuitive "knowing" that everything is happening according to plan, regardless of appearance. There would be no reason to get angry or to be fearful or pessimistic because everything is arriving right on schedule.

You might say, "You don't know what my job is like. There is no way in the world I could do this—I have too much pressure." You might say, "You don't understand what my friends are like. I deal with so much frustration trying to live up to their expectations and the expectations of my family—you just don't understand."

Yes, I do. But we are talking about *one* day. In fact, the way that your friends and family behave is likely none of your business. Ask yourself why you are reacting the way you are to their actions. Could the root partially be in your own insecurity? Is there a hidden lesson that you can learn about yourself?

When you are able to get to the point where your life, well-being, and character is seldom affected by the turbulence that is going on around you, then life as you know it will change forever. There will be no need for other people to "make" you happy. There will be no dependency on peoples' attitudes to make *your* attitude what you want it to be.

Let me remind you of this, however: Regardless of the day which you choose to live gratefully, there will be difficult times. There will be times where we each may have small losses—and times when we may have large losses. It is inevitable. In difficult times, you will still feel strong emotion, but the difference is that you will now have the tools to deal with these emotions in an empowering new way. You will see the challenges and you will rise to the challenges, though it will sometimes feel much easier than others.

On this grateful day, there will be no need for other people to conform to your way of thinking because your thoughts, actions, attitudes, and responses will strictly be based on your choices. There will be no worry about the way people will act toward you in certain situations because your actions will be straight from the heart, in alignment with the core traits that you hold so dear.

For this day when you are living as the type of person that you want—and choose—to be, manipulation has little or no effect on you. When you are being the type of person you want to be, the moods of others have little or no effect on you. It's no longer your responsibility or burden to make another person happy. You simply live out your life with a powerful, authentic presence and it is clear to yourself and to everyone that you are confident with the person you have become. You're able to step back and look at the big picture in a wise way, and you are less likely to get caught up in the drama that tempts us in our daily lives.

Now that you know what you want, instead of what you don't want, it's time to leave the theoretical vacuum of what *might* be and enter the arena for the great game of the day that *will* be. It's time to put it all together and live one grateful day. Ignore excuses that begin entering your head such as, "This will be impossible," "There is no time for that stuff," or (my all-time least favorite excuse) "If I had an easier/higher paying/more glamorous/more flexible job, I could do it."

I would offer that if you have one of these challenging scenarios above, congratulations! You're a perfect candidate to enter into one day of gratitude. As usual, you will have to choose your attitude of gratitude, and if you can choose this attitude under challenging conditions, then there is nothing in life that can stop you.

At some point when you make this decision to achieve your goal in a trusting and persistent way, you will find doors almost magically begin to open and people will be there to help you reach those goals. Remember this each time you see it happen, because on many days of this journey you will likely feel as if you are going two steps forward and three steps backward. You will likely wake up, choose a good, grateful mindset, and then one hour later "decide" (always a choice) to be ungrateful.

Something will happen that is not according to your plan. The good news is that at some point you will learn that even those frustrating times of perceived failure can be quickly trumped when you cover them with gratitude. Here is more good news: The quicker you acknowledge that there is something in everything to be grateful for, the quicker it becomes that way…permanently.

Here are a few more tips about things to do as your day begins. First, clear up as many energy zappers as you can, because in our lives we are consciously and unconsciously surrounded by inefficient, resentment-producing, contentment-stealing pollutants. They creep in, and we often don't even realize that it has happened until it's too late and we are pulled into a power-draining, ungrateful mire and left to fend off the demons.

The foods we are eating, the people we are associating with, the words we choose, the organization of our work and leisure spaces—all of these choices create an environment in which gratitude may flourish or in which gratitude is diminished. If the people you are associating with are consistently using language that is discouraging or envious or gossip-oriented, you will find it to be an ongoing struggle to infuse your conversations with gratitude. If you are regularly consuming foods that you know are not healthy, you will essentially be putting oil in the gas tank of your gratitude vehicle. If your work space or leisure areas are disorganized, you will have a more challenging time being focused on your task at hand because it will seem as if all of the items lying around you are calling to you to deal with them.

As you surround yourself with these pollutants, you can't help but resonate with them. The result is that your potential for feeling grateful in the great game of life is dramatically decreased. As you look through those lenses, you start seeing more and more of what's *not* working. Gratitude now becomes unnecessarily difficult.

In *Power vs. Force*, Dr. David Hawkins similarly explains the importance of surrounding yourself with good (or gratitude) in terms of what he calls energy or attractor patterns. He writes, "Success comes as the automatic consequence of aligning one's life with high-power energy patterns."[1] According to Dr. Hawkins, the more we create an environment which is in alignment with these powerful attractor patterns, the more that goodness and successful outcomes become a part of our lives—a type of inevitable magnetic attraction.

Gratitude overcomes negativity and changes the filters we look through. We can then begin applying thankfulness to…everything. To people, places, words, actions, and situations.

Lastly, as you immerse yourself into this one full day of gratitude, be prepared. There are going to be some intriguing things that happen. First of all, as you have some success, you are going to feel as if you have found a great secret to a richer life—which, by the way, you have. Secondly, you're going to be more aware of how often *you* tend to make pessimistic comments or react in less than constructive ways. Thirdly, you're going to be aware of those same tendencies in others. With your awareness raised, you'll get the feeling that something is definitely different here. You will realize you are on the right path.

So now, let's take a look at what one day of living fully grateful will be like. It will start by waking up and making a conscious effort to smile. That's right, smile. You may even have to take your index fingers and pull the corners of your mouth up at first, but just do it. When you start off the day with even a slight smile, you lay the groundwork for a lot more smiles. The tendency, quite often, is to wake up wishing things were different—like having more sleep, a different job, warmer temperatures, a shorter commute, and on and on.

Once you choose to wake up and smile, pile on the goodness by saying to yourself how grateful you are for one thing you see as you walk through your surroundings. For example, "I'm grateful for the beautiful hardwood floor I am walking on." As you begin your routine, the challenges/opportunities will be close by. Now is a good time to start looking for the game and the personal challenge in what otherwise would be your "problems" for the upcoming day.

This is where it really gets fun. If you're expecting to have the world simply cooperate with your quest for a day of gratitude, don't. Well, that actually isn't quite true. The world *will* cooperate with you, on its own terms. It will give you all the lessons and opportunities you'll need to develop a rock-solid, grateful state of being. What it won't do is change either people or situations to suit your agenda and help you reach your goal of being fully grateful all day long.

In fact, if it did, what would you have really accomplished? Not much. Other people and experiences would have done all the changing, and, as we said earlier, the change must begin with us. This is a key concept in our journey to gratefulness, and when you completely believe this, you're already well on your way to not one day of gratitude—but a lifetime of gratitude in all situations.

Yet, I digress. Our day continues as we move through our morning. You may very well see that the weather is cloudy or rainy or that it may be hailing. But having a fully grateful day means seeing beyond the weather. Instead, you happily choose to see the weather as you would see the background of a spectacular play. It's simply a setting for the scene, not the scene itself. It's the playing field that you happen to be on that day—nothing more, nothing less.

As you go to work or school, or wherever your next stop is, you take full, deep breaths and look for what is right. Look for the beauty of your surroundings. Look for the good in whomever you meet. When you pass people on the road or in the hallways, you remember that each of them have their own painful challenges that they are dealing with. With this attitude, it becomes much easier to see throughout your day that very few comments or insults are really personally directed toward you. The comments are typically made out of insecurity, fear, misunderstanding, or all of the above—and it's not your job to change them. It's your job to simply pursue your vision of excellence and dispassionately let the chips fall where they may. Keep looking for the game that can be played in different scenarios—the game will be there if you creatively seek it.

As the obstacles and "teachers" continue to cross your path and you feel the oncoming emotions, continue to breathe deeply. When conflict appears on the horizon, remember to stay on the playing field and stay away from the battlefield. Remind yourself to have no complaints as you learn the lessons and prepare yourself for even better days ahead. Gratitude trumps everything—and everything that happens is practice for being consistently grateful.

Again, when you look at it this way, there can be no failure!

As the day continues, periodically reflect on your word choices. Look for opportunities to use your new vocabulary of gratitude. Use words like *hope, optimism, trust, believe, good, yes, opportunity,* and *fun*. As much as possible, avoid words or phrases such as *got to, need to, terrible, never,* or *awful*. Not only do these words make you feel ungrateful, they cast you in the role of a victim, and they make the people around you feel ungrateful.

You may "do" activities or you may "want to do" activities, so typically choose those types of empowering words because "having to do" something (as we'll discuss later) portrays your reality as you having no choice in the matter, which can lead to resentment, frustration, and pessimism.

Look for chances throughout your day to express your gratitude and appreciation for specific, genuine attributes of the people you encounter. It is beyond powerful; it is a "game-changer." It makes you feel good, and it makes the recipients feel good—it's just a win-win.

Additionally, what you will notice as the day continues is that you have been essentially *creating* an environment that is conducive to feeling good, optimistic, and grateful. Your new perspective has begun shaping your reality because gratitude has been a priority all during your day. Keep breathing slowly, gently, and fully—no pressing or forcing today.

As you meet people throughout your day, smile. There's nothing that reflects gratitude more than a genuine smile. When we give a heartfelt smile it says to the person you encounter, "I like you and I like me." The connection that is made when we smile is one based on unselfishness, vulnerability, kindness, and peace. These characteristics get ingrained in you, and then they become contagious.

Again, the temptation to be less than grateful will accost you.

Here's an interesting example of how your view of the day can subtly drift away from playing the game with gratitude: I was walking out of the gym around seven thirty one warm summer morning and a gentleman of around sixty years was getting into his truck. He saw me and glumly greeted me with, "Too pretty to go to work today. Be a lot better going fishing."

I laughed and countered, "Yep, guess you need to figure out how to turn work into play today!"

"Hmmm, maybe when I retire I can fish," he grumbled.

What this man did unconsciously was to set himself up to think of work as "no fun" or somewhere he didn't want to be. This type of attitude creates resistance and a subtle form of ongoing resentment. It puts work and play in the context of mutual exclusiveness, whereas gratitude bridges the gap between the two. (Granted, sometimes a job is so miserable that we must look somewhere else for employment and fulfillment. Just first ask, "Have I learned the lessons I needed to learn about myself, and how I may have contributed to this misery?")

You may say, "Maybe he just wanted to be outside in the nice weather." Nope, he was in construction, so he worked outside. What's also important to understand from this interaction is this: It's typically our relationship to our work that causes us stress, not the work itself. You may also say, he was just kidding, but remember that your word is your wand, and words often precipitate what will come to pass.

It's worth reiterating that you may feel as if you are failing again and again throughout the day. However, I would like to remind you that every time you respond to your perceived failure with an element of gratitude for the lessons to be learned and for the growth that you are experiencing, you're winning the game! You're affirming your power of awareness, acceptance, and strength that you are gaining—and you are also easing the stress, tension, and guilt that we tend to get when we feel we have missed the mark.

"Oh man, this is going to be hard, I can tell," you may be thinking. Well, maybe. Or maybe you can look at it as the Frenchman Émile Coué did, when he commented, "Always think of what you have to do as easy, and it will become so."[2] I would frequently offer to my children when they were younger that "it's not a big deal unless you make it a big deal," and more often than not, that is the case. This is also your day to reflect on some of the other characteristics we've talked about that go along with a spirit of gratitude: patience, encouragement, enthusiasm, persistence, and gentleness. Throughout your day, notice how many opportunities come into your life to allow you to practice and share so many of these traits. Also, notice how you feel each time you incorporate one of them into your actions. An undeniable energy is released that affects not only you, but also those around you—an energy that is quickly transferred to people that your chosen "gratitude beneficiaries" later come into contact with. The ripple effect begins with you.

Buy someone a cup of coffee or tea, for example, and then listen to the hurts and joys of someone you normally don't spend much time with. Cheer or give credit to people in your life who have had major or minor successes. Hold off before you react to perceived criticism and give thanks where you would typically give skepticism. Laugh when you would possibly tend to be stone-faced or stoic.

By late afternoon, you will no doubt have had many opportunities to connect with others through gratitude. Put some icing on the cake of this one grateful day: take some time in the early evening to write to someone who would really benefit from receiving a note of appreciation. You could also take a moment and reach out with a phone call or an email to someone who has made a difference in your life. But take care that you write the note or speak with genuine appreciation for this person's accomplishment or action. As we said earlier, a compliment that is given insincerely is simply a controlling gesture thinly disguised as praise, and neither party receives the benefits that actually would come from an honest sentiment.

As you write or talk, take your time and be as precise with your words as possible. Picture that person in your mind and feel the gratitude that you have for them and for what it is you are recognizing about them.

Once you have finished, move on to your next task and have no expectations of acknowledgment from the person. The temptation to expect a quick return on your grateful investment is a trap we want to stay out of. As my friend Ken Guy astutely says, "Be careful where you expect your rewards to come from." In this case, the purity of the task will be its own reward, and anything else will be a bonus.

When your day comes to a close, look back for ways to appreciate the events that occurred through the day. Each of them worked together to provide fertile ground for your spiritual improvement, so be thankful that it happened just as it did and know that you have gained wisdom through the trials that have been put in front of you. Congratulations, my friend. You have just taken a tremendous step toward permanently being a champion in playing the great game of life with gratitude—and the best is yet to come!

---

[1] David R. Hawkins, *Power vs. Force: The Hidden Determinants of Human Behavior* (Carlsbad, CA: Hay House, 2012), 206.
[2] Maxwell Maltz, *Psycho-Cybernetics: A New Way to Get More Living Out of Life* (New York: Pocket Books, 1989), 75.

Chapter 11
The Never-Ending Path: Becoming a Master in Living the Grateful Life

The Master in the Art of Living makes no distinction between his work and his play, his labor and his leisure, his mind and his body, his information and his recreation, his life and his religion. He simply pursues his vision of excellence at whatever he does, leaving others to decide whether he is working or playing. To him, he is always doing both.

– James Michener

A master in the way of gratitude is much like this master in the art of living to whom Michener refers. For each of them, gratefulness has not only been ingrained in their actions, it has permeated the core of their being.

Stephen Mitchell, in his book *The Second Book of the Tao*, speaks of this rare person as he comments, "He understands that nothing is absolute, that since every point of view depends on the viewer, affirmation and denial are equally beside the point."[1]

Gratitude masters know the unselfish power and potential that is available in a life filled with appreciation and trust, regardless of how the situation may appear to others. As you progress in your practice, you will find yourself evolving toward this stage of mastery, in some extremely significant ways. It will, indeed, likely be an evolution. And to the degree that you see maturity in these areas, you will not only understand intellectually that gratitude has become a habitual part of you, you will *know* that you have transcended patterns that you did not even realize were holding you back from a freer, more grateful life.

Most significantly, you will find that you have developed an ability to positively impact others in a meaningful way. This skill to influence peoples' lives for the better will come from who you have become through your experience, not what you particularly *do*. It's a natural outgrowth that has far reaching branches of goodness. Here are some of the markers to let you know you're reaching a stage of excellence in your journey:

1. The distinction between "have tos" and "want tos" is increasingly blurred.

2. The process has become more important than the outcome.

3. Your environment has become conducive to gratefulness.

1. The distinction between "have tos" and "want tos" is increasingly blurred. You will find that life becomes more about seeing everything as "perfectly fine," just as it is. Tennis legend

Arthur Ashe addressed this when he spoke of his battle with terminal illness:

> If I ask "Why me?" as I am assaulted by heart disease and AIDS, I must ask 'Why me?' about my blessings and question my right to enjoy them. The morning after I won Wimbledon in 1975 I should have asked "Why me?" and doubted that I deserved the victories. If I don't ask "Why me?" after my victories, I cannot ask "Why me?" after my setbacks and distresses.[2]

Arthur Ashe was the epitome of a grateful man—an expert in the art. He had reached the point where he personified the understanding that acceptable or unacceptable are in the eye of the beholder. If you ever saw Arthur Ashe compete on the professional tennis tour, you saw a person who exuded grace, humility, and a gratitude for the sport he had chosen. His skill in the game was akin to a craftsman who loved his work so much he never dared perform in a way that might diminish the view of it by anyone. Therefore, he competed every time with nothing less than grace, dignity, and pure joy for the opportunities he was afforded in his craft.

As this view of what's okay or not okay fades, then, proportionally, life's tasks that "have to" be done, now become grateful possibilities in your daily landscape.

2. The process has become more important than the outcome. Our fearful tendencies to try to control our future and relive our past are "gratitude killers." A person who has grown to see potential for gratitude in everything has learned to gradually let go of those tendencies. This person understands that each task and interaction is worthy of attention and appreciation at that moment. Eckhart Tolle comments:

> Don't look for peace. Don't look for any other state than the one you are in now; otherwise, you will set up inner conflict and unconscious resistance. Forgive yourself for not being at peace. The moment you completely accept your non-peace, your non-peace becomes transmuted into peace. Anything you accept fully will get you there, will take you into peace. This is the miracle of surrender.[3]

Focusing on gratitude each moment has the same result.

Learning to focus on the process instead of the outcome is actually a manifestation of faith, and, as we have said, faith and gratitude go hand in hand. To a mature student in gratitude, a "successful" outcome is simply a by-product of a trusting, grateful, full participation in the quality of one's tasks. The conclusion becomes less and less anxiously anticipated as the doer of the deed essentially merges with the work, thus creating a task-oriented authenticity that leads to a magnificent result.

Joseph Jaworski, in *Synchronicity: The Inner Path of Leadership,* comments on the opening of doors that begins at this point, as he writes, "When we are in this state of being where we are open to life and all its possibilities, willing to take the next step as it is presented to us, then we meet the most remarkable people who are important contributors to our life."[4]

3. Your environment has become conducive to gratefulness. As you continue on the gratitude trek, you will notice that you have the tendency to surround yourself with people who are grateful. As we discussed earlier, these types of relationships are conducive to your new or renewed way of living, and so you'll find them appearing more in your life. As you connect more with encouraging and thankful people, you will feel better and your grateful sphere of influence will spread even more broadly. People who are pessimistic and typically unappreciative will not resonate with you, and you will notice that they harmoniously fade from your life.

As I shared earlier, you may also see that you gravitate more toward optimistic, uplifting sayings, poems, or stories. You may notice as you reach this more advanced stage that you have the desire to purge your surroundings of old pictures or items that simply do not "speak" to you as they previously had. Organizing and updating your space is healthy anyway, but clearing away clutter and replacing it with things that reflect gratitude and goodness gives you a clear head and a lighter spirit that will help allow you to feel happily in control of your environment, instead of toxically enslaved by it.

You'll be aware that there are shops, homes, and generally places that you go that indescribably feel right to you, as do appreciative words that people choose. The filters of gratitude tend to affect every part of your life. You have, to a great extent, "become" gratitude, and so your ability to sense everything and everyone that has an element of gratefulness has, in turn, become extremely acute.

You may think that all these transformational actions require you to do a great deal of work to achieve them—and you could successfully argue that point. But, on the other hand, when it comes to changing habits, it more likely seems that there actually is an element of ease involved. Author Dr. Maxwell Maltz adds, "Our currently held beliefs, whether good or bad, true or false, were formed *without effort*, with no sense of strain, and without the exercise of 'willpower.' Our habits, whether good or bad, were formed in the same way. It follows that we must employ the same process in forming new beliefs, or new habits, that is, in a relaxed condition."[5]

Maltz also points to research by the late Dr. Knight Dunlap, who made a lifelong study of habits and learning processes. Wrote Maltz: "His methods succeeded in curing such habits as nail-biting, thumb-sucking, facial tics, and more serious habits where other methods had failed. The very heart of his system was his finding that effort was the one big deterrent to either breaking a bad habit, or learning a new one. Making an effort to refrain from the habit actually reinforced the habit, he found. His experiments proved that the best way to break a habit is to form a clear mental image of the desired end result, and to practice, without effort, moving toward that goal."[6]

To amplify this discussion and put it in the context of gratitude growth: The path toward reaching the level of being fully grateful for everything might be compared to an attempt to excel in a sport, because, like a sport, achieving a level of excellence in the game of gratitude takes desire, goal-setting, and the ability to patiently, persistently work through the obstacles in one's path. However, relative to Dr. Maltz's comments, a level of mastery can be reached in gratitude practice in a way that is different than the way it is achieved in athletics. In the gratitude realm, at a certain point, willful effort essentially becomes a thing of the past. It is replaced by a grateful state of being that is imperturbable and capable of impacting the world primarily through presence. The gratitude pilgrim at this point has been transformed and thankfulness pervades his or her life.

It doesn't mean that improvement stops. It doesn't mean that focus on the goal stops, and it doesn't mean that prayer and meditation stop. But now, development has entered a new stage. Dr. Deepak Chopra speaks to this point as he quotes an ancient Indian adage in his book *The Soul of Leadership*: "This isn't knowledge that you learn. It's knowledge that you become."[7]

At this stage we gently, consistently, patiently allow things to unfold for ourselves and for others. Through the continued experience of unending gratitude, we fully understand that life is happening just as it should—and it's a cause for celebration.

Now, you may again be thinking, "I will never get *there*." Again, like our pilgrim in the earlier story, you must first have the desire to get to the top of the mountain, and then you must persevere in order to see the reward. The following is a reminder I wrote for all of us on this journey. It speaks of the opportunities available every day to grow our gratefulness to extraordinary levels, regardless of the situation:

See the Good in Everything

See the good in all that enters your life. Every seemingly stressful or difficult situation,

or interaction, is an opportunity to work spiritually on an undeveloped portion of you.

If you feel resentment, it is an opportunity to work on kindness.

If you feel anger, it is a chance to work on gentleness.

If you feel anxious, it is a chance to work on acceptance.

If you feel fear, it is a chance to work on faith.

If you feel neglected, it is a chance to work on patience.

If you feel sadness, it is a chance to work on appreciation.

When you trust that life is happening exactly as it should, you can gratefully let

go and allow the right way to reveal itself.

At this point, it's important to note that simply because you have been blessed to reach a degree of mastery in gratitude and appreciation for events in your life, opportunities to regress loom close by. With all the beautiful benefits of this new view of life, the master knows that impostors such as fear, loneliness, confusion, discrimination, and disappointment are still awaiting the chance to recover what they seemingly have lost.

The game does not get easier, so consider this level of difficulty and these obstacles you have encountered as supreme, noble tests of your developing skill. In fact, you may find that the higher your skill level becomes, the more complex the challenges you may face.

The master welcomes these challenges as one would welcome a good friend. The grateful, trusting person knows that the ensuing results will be appropriate even when you don't know exactly what these outcomes will be. Likewise, your ability to think and act in these terms will be representative of the fact that the game has changed and you are more than ready to play it.

The appearance of new levels of obstacles will be increasingly overcome by your calm, confident, grateful spirit, which addresses these challenges one at a time. A vivid memory I have of this type of mastery is from an event which occurred when I was a teenager. I was competing one summer in a tennis tournament that was extremely important to me as a competitive athlete. Halfway through this match, which my mother had come to watch, my opponent and I took a mandatory break as we prepared to play toward the conclusion.

I was, at the time, a highly-ranked player in my state and expected to win this particular match in suburban Atlanta over a much lower-ranked opponent—but it wasn't happening on this day. In fact, the momentum had shifted, and I was on the losing end of it, no matter what I tried to do. As we took a rest, I began some serious catastrophe thinking and started pondering what would happen to my ranking if I lost this match.

Sitting there as the sweltering, Georgia sun beat down on me into the late afternoon, I began to think about losing my opportunity to earn a college tennis scholarship—something I had worked for since I was ten years old by practicing hours and hours every day. This had been my best year yet, and now, at the end of the season, I was in danger of it all falling apart.

As I went and sat by my mom, I felt embarrassed—not only because I was losing a match that she came to see, but upset that I was on the verge of crying as I sat beside her. To be fighting back tears when seeing Mom is not what an adolescent athlete wants to have happen.

But then, a most touching, memorable thing took place: My mother looked down at me with a serene smile on her face, put her arm around me and said, "Skipper, it's all going to be okay—you're going to do just fine. You go out there and do what you can do, and I'm going to sit right here while you play the best you can today, and it's going to be just fine."

Whether my mom believed that or not, her actions and tone could not have appeared any more sincere to me. As she looked into my eyes, there was a gentleness, a kindness, a strength, and a spirit of compassion that were beyond words. It was the personification of gratitude. She was grateful for life, grateful to be with me, grateful to be sharing my struggle, and grateful—ahead of time—for the outcome, whatever it might be.

I returned to the court and put my heart into that final hour at a level that surprised even me. And in case you're wondering, I did win the match. But in retrospect, I am not sure that really was the important part of that day. What I do know is that my mother's ability to transfer her faith and gratitude to me that day has been indelibly etched in my mind. I now know that a presence of authentic gratitude and compassion can impact someone when words really are secondary issues. Her heartfelt gratitude wasn't dependent on the successful completion of my effort. It was appreciation related to my *being*—not to my *doing*, and I felt it. This type of gratitude contains and transfers power that is unique, and it knows no limitation.

Remember, as we work toward this level of gratitude excellence, we may still feel a lack of confidence and a discomfort in our practice of these skills. But that should happen less and less, and the recovery time becomes much quicker each time we miss the mark in our attempts. Plus, each time you succeed in shifting from insecurity, reactiveness, defensiveness, or impatience to gentleness and gratefulness, you affirm your resolve to pursue the attitude of gratitude and of seeing life as a great game.

Keep in mind that mastery happens incrementally. It happens often in glimpses of what *could* be. However, do know this: The path to this success, though fraught with potential difficulties and what often seems to be unseen and thankless effort, will reward you and others in many life-enhancing ways. It shapes and empowers and causes ripple effects that produce incalculable, long-term effects that will live on for years to come.

---

[1] Stephen Mitchell, *The Second Book of the Tao* (New York: Penguin Books, 2010), 12.
[2] Arthur Ashe, *Days of Grace* (New York: Ballantine Books, 1994), 462.
[3] Eckhart Tolle, *The Power of Now: A Guide to Spiritual Enlightenment* (Novato, CA: New World Library, 2004), 160–161.
[4] Joseph Jaworski, *Synchronicity: The Inner Path of Leadership* (San Francisco: Berrett-Koehler Publishers, 2011), 49.
[5] Maxwell Maltz, *Psycho-Cybernetics: A New Way to Get More Living Out of Life* (New York: Pocket Books, 1989), 59.
[6] Ibid., 59–60.
[7] Deepak Chopra, *The Soul of Leadership: Unlocking Your Potential for Greatness* (New York: Harmony Books, 2010), 68.

Chapter 12
The Choice

I shall be telling this with a sigh

Somewhere ages and ages hence:

Two roads diverged in a wood, and I,

I took the one less traveled by,

And that has made all the difference.

— Robert Frost, "The Road Not Taken"

So, it comes down to this: As your expedition to a fully empowered life of gratitude reaches its destination at the top of the mountain, as our pilgrim's did, how will you choose? Will you choose to see your world through lenses of gratitude and appreciation, and life as the great game to be played, or will you choose to see your world through the lenses of impossibility, fear, and despair on the "battlefield"?

You may slice it any way you'd like, but the question still remains, "How will you choose in the various situations that will confront you?"

Our tendency may be to want to blame life on someone else and say we don't have the time, ability, resources, or energy to live with gratitude every day. But when we strip away all the excuses, the playing field is extremely level, and life waits patiently for us to take it by the reins and choose to lean on the shoulder of gratitude.

You now have the tools, and you have scaled the mountain on your expedition. As I leave you to now stand at the top and prepare for the return journey to practice gratitude on your own, thoughtfully review the following poem. Although it was more than five years ago, I vividly remember sitting on a beach during a colorful sunset in Ocho Rios, Jamaica, with my then teen-aged daughters. I was sharing this poem with them, which I had written for my daughter Betsy's high school graduation. I believe its message is still as applicable today as it was then, and I would like to close this book with that piece, which I call "The Choice." It serves as a reminder that our ability to choose to gratefully live and love the great game daily is one of the most beautiful and meaningful gifts that we possess:

The Choice

Regardless of the way I approach it, I will reach the end of this day.
I can get there by approaching each task and interaction in a relaxed, trusting way,
Or I can get there in an anxious, fearful way;
The choice is mine, no one else's.
I can get there in a gentle, grateful way,
Or I can get there in a harsh, resentful way;
The choice is mine, no one else's.
I can get there with beliefs of optimism and abundance,

Or I can get there with beliefs of pessimism and scarcity;

The choice is mine, no one else's.

I can give confidently and generously, expecting no return,

Or I can chase the illusion of control by measuring out favor and carefully keeping score;

The choice is mine, no one else's.

I can get there by seeing challenges as steps toward reaching my goals,

Or I can get there by seeing them as overwhelming problems that may cause me to fail;

The choice is mine, no one else's.

Life will be a beautiful, continuously unfolding adventure today,

Or it will be a dreary, monotonous journey;

That choice will always be mine, no one else's.

Bibliography

Alabama. "I'm In A Hurry (And Don't Know Why)." *American Pride*. 1992.

Anxiety and Depression Association of America. "Facts and Statistics." Last modified November 2012. http://www.adaa.org/about-adaa/press-room/facts-statistics.

Ashe, Arthur. *Days of Grace*. New York: Ballantine Books, 1994.

Beattie, Melody. *Codependent No More*. Center City, MN: Hazelden, 1992.

Belitz, Charlene, and Meg Lundstrom. *The Power of Flow: Practical Ways to Transform Your Life with Meaningful Coincidence*. New York: Three Rivers Press, 1998.

"Blind Hiker Finishes 8-Month Trek on Appalachian Trail." *The Washington Times*. November 22, 1991.

Bush, Sr., George. "Inaugural Address." January 20, 1989. http://www.britannica.com/presidents/article-9116858.

Caruso, Joe. *The Power of Losing Control: Finding Strength, Meaning, and Happiness in an Out-of-Control World*. Grosse Ile, MI: Brookshire Press, 2003.

Chödrön, Pema. *Comfortable with Uncertainty: 108 Teachings on Cultivating Fearlessness and Compassion*. Boston: Shambhala Publications, 2003.

Chopra, Deepak. *The Soul of Leadership: Unlocking Your Potential for Greatness*. New York: Harmony Books, 2010.

Covey, Stephen R. *Principle-Centered Leadership*. New York: Fireside, 1992.

Dr. Seuss, *Oh, the Places You'll Go!* New York: Random House, 1990.

Emerson, Ralph Waldo. *The Complete Works of Ralph Waldo Emerson*. Boston: Houghton Mifflin Company, 1904.

Frankl, Viktor E. *Man's Search for Meaning*. Boston: Beacon Press, 2006.

Garner, Eric. *The A to Z of Presentations*. Telluride, CO: Ventus Publishing, 2012.

Hammarskjöld, Dag. *Markings*. New York: Ballantine Books, 1985.

Harpo, Inc. "Condoleezza Rice's *Master Class* Quotes." Last modified February 13, 2011. http://www.oprah.com/own-master-class/Condoleezza-Rices-Master-Class-Quotes.

Hawkins, David R. *Power vs. Force: The Hidden Determinants of Human Behavior*. Carlsbad, CA: Hay House, 2012.

Howe, Randy, ed. *The Yankees Fanatic*. Guilford, CT: Lyons Press, 2007.

Jaworski, Joseph. *Synchronicity: The Inner Path of Leadership*. San Francisco: Berrett-Koehler Publishers, 2011.

Keller, Helen. *The Open Door*. New York: Doubleday, 1957.

Lieberman, David J. *Make Peace With Anyone: Breakthrough Strategies to Quickly End Any Conflict, Feud, or Estrangement*. New York: St. Martin's Griffin, 2003.

Maltz, Maxwell. *Psycho-Cybernetics: A New Way to Get More Living Out of Life*. New York: Pocket Books, 1989.

Mitchell, Stephen. *The Second Book of the Tao*. New York: Penguin Books, 2010.

Nelson, Bob. *1001 Ways to Reward Employees*. New York: Workman Publishing Company, 2005.

Nietzsche, Friedrich. *Basic Writings of Nietzsche*. Translated by Walter Kaufmann. New York: Modern Library, 2000.

Page, Susan. "Don't Say 'No' to South Carolina Gov. Nikki Haley." *USA Today*, April 03, 2012.

Quote Investigator. "Watch Your Thoughts." Last modified January 10, 2013. http://quoteinvestigator.com/2013/01/10/watch-your-thoughts.

Robinson, Peter. *How Ronald Reagan Changed My Life*. New York: Harper Perennial, 2004.

Saint Francis de Sales. BrainyQuote.com. Xplore, Inc. Last modified 2013. http://www.brainyquote.com/quotes/quotes/s/saintfranc193305.html.

Saraceno, Jon. "Tyson: 'My Whole Life has been a Waste.'" *USA Today*, June 02, 2005.

Shibayama, Abbott Zenkei. *A Flower Does Not Talk: Zen Essays*. North Clarendon, VT: Tuttle Publishing, 1971.

Shinn, Florence Scovel. *The Wisdom of Florence Scovel Shinn*. New York: Fireside, 1989.

———. *Your Word is Your Wand*. Radford, VA: Wilder Publications, 2009.

Tolle, Eckhart. *The Power of Now: A Guide to Spiritual Enlightenment*. Novato, CA: New World Library, 2004.

———. *Stillness Speaks*. Novato, CA: New World Library, 2003.

About the Author

Skip Johnson is the Vice President of Operations at Gold's Gyms of West Georgia, based in Douglasville, Georgia. The businesses have been the recipients of over twenty state, sectional, national, and international awards, including Best Customer Service worldwide. Skip has also been designated by the United States Professional Tennis Association as a Master Tennis Professional—a level achieved by less than 1 percent of the more than 15,000 certified tennis pros.

In addition to his writing, Skip has a passion for speaking, and he conducts workshops and gives presentations on diverse topics such as personal development, leadership, tennis business and instructional excellence, company and program organization, and customer satisfaction. He and his wife Anne Marie love to travel, find fun experiences, and share time with old friends while meeting new friends along the way. They live outside of Atlanta, Georgia, and have four daughters (and a few dogs and cats).

Skip may be reached at www.facebook.com/SkipJohnsonAuthor.